iPhone 14
USER GUIDE

GW00392476

The Most Comprehensive and Intuitive Guide on How to Use Your New iPhone 14 With Tips and Tricks, from Beginner to Advanced User

Jeff Young

Table of Contents

INTRODUCTION

This book has been prepared for beginners and seniors. It has the latest tips and tricks to help iPhone 14 users master and use their devices like experts.

If you're switching from Android smartphones and other devices to the iPhone for the first time, this guide has you covered.

This book has pictures and step-by-step instructions to help you improve and fast-track your mastery of the iPhone 14, 14 Plus, 14 Pro, and 14 Pro Max, its features, and its usage.

Features of iPhone 14 Series

The iPhone 14 and 14 Plus

The iPhone 14 and 14 Plus are the most recent affordable smartphones from Apple in the iPhone 14 lineup. The company has discontinued the "Mini" version. Both models have screen sizes of 6.1 and 6.7 inches. The two devices are similar to the iPhone 13 models in that they have flat edges, an aerospace-grade aluminum chassis, and a glass back that allows for wireless charging.

The iPhone 14 and 14 Plus are available in five colors: midnight, blue, purple, starlight, and red.

Both devices retain the notch at the front of the screen, which houses the TrueDepth camera, as opposed to the 14 Pro models, which have the notch replaced with "Display Island."

The devices feature a Super Retina XDR OLED screen with up to 1200 nits of peak brightness, Dolby Vision, and True Tone, which adjusts the screen's white balance to the background lighting. Unlike the Pro models, the iPhone 14 and 14 Plus do not have ProMotion display technology.

The screen of the iPhone is shielded by a durable Ceramic Shield front cover, and the device is IP68 water resistant, allowing submersion at a depth of 6 meters for up to thirty minutes.

Both low-cost models use the A15 chip, also used in the iPhone 13 lineup. On the other hand, Apple has improved internal design to allow for better thermal performance. The processor has a six-core CPU, a five-core GPU, and a sixteen-core Neural Engine.

Apple has added an improved 12-MP Wide camera with a larger sensor, a /1.5 aperture, larger 1.9 m pixels for improved performance in low-light situations, and sensor-shift optical image stabilization. They've also included an improved TrueDepth camera with a /1.9 aperture, and while the Ultrawide lens hasn't been updated, the Photonic Engine technology improves low-light photography when using the camera app.

Apple has also added Action Mode when recording videos to provide a polished look with improved photo stabilization. Don't worry if you need to record a video in the middle of the action; Action Mode can compensate for severe shaking, movements, and vibrations. Cinematic Mode has also been improved, allowing you to record in 4K at 30 frames per second (fps) and 4K at 24 fps. Surprisingly, the True Tone flash is now 10% brighter and more consistent.

A dual-core accelerometer, accelerometer, and a high dynamic range gyroscope power the new Crash Detection feature, which helps to contact emergency services if you're involved in a serious accident and can't reach your iPhone. The barometer analyzes changes in cabin pressure, the GPS sensor monitors speed variations, and the microphone detects impact sounds similar to car crashes. This feature is also available in iPhone 14 Pro models.

For the first time, the Cupertino-based company has included Satellite Emergency SOS. This feature allows your iPhone to communicate with satellites when Wi-Fi and cellular networks are unavailable.

The Emergency SOS through satellite works in an open space without obstructing trees and lets you send texts to the emergency service. For now, it will only be available in the U.S. and Canada. In the Find My app, you can also use satellite connectivity to share your location with your pals and loved ones. As expected, this feature is also available in the Pro models

The iPhone 14 models support 5G connectivity. In the US, the device comes with an eSIM, while other regions can still ship with a physical SIM card slot. Apple has also improved the battery life of the iPhone 14. Both phones support MagSafe charging up to 15W and fast charging through Lightning with a 20W or higher charger.

It offers three storage options: 128GB, 256GB, and 512GB storage capacities. Both devices also support Wi-Fi 6 and Bluetooth 5.3.

The iPhone 14 Pro and 14 Pro Max

The iPhone 14 Pro and iPhone 14 Pro Max were unveiled alongside the cheaper iPhone 14 and iPhone 14 Plus. The Pro model offers more rich features than the iPhone 14 models, ranging from improved camera technology, an enhanced

display, an even faster A16 processor, etc.

The iPhone 14 Pro has a 6.1-inch screen, while the Pro Max comes with a 6.7-inch. Both devices feature flat edges, a stainless-steel casing, IP68 water resistance, textured matte glass at the back, and a Ceramic Shield for screen protection. It now has a larger camera bump to house the new lenses, and there are changes on display.

Apple has removed the notch that houses the TrueDepth camera technology and has rather adopted what the company called "Dynamic Island," which is a pill-shaped hole at the front of the phone's screen that contains the camera system and can get bigger or smaller, depending on what's showing on your screen.

The "Dynamic Island" now shows phone calls, reminders, timers, notifications, map directions, and activities in the location where the notch used to be.

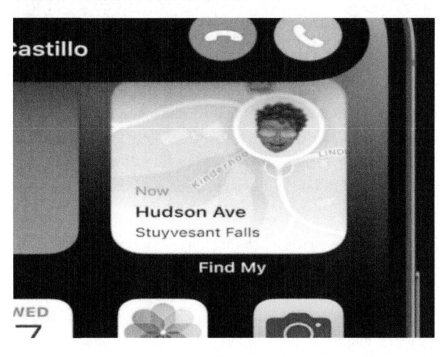

Both devices have a refreshed Super Retina XDR display with improved ProMotion technology and an Always-On display. Your wallpaper is dimmed while the widgets, time, and other live activities are still available when Always-On Display is turned on. The screen also offers a maximum HDR brightness of up to 2000 nits.

The iPhone 14 Pro models are powered by the new A16 processor, which offers speed and performance improvements. The processor has a six-core CPU, an accelerated five-core GPU with 50% additional memory bandwidth, and a refreshed sixteen-core Neural Engine, which can complete 17 trillion operations per second.

The Pro models now have a 48-MP wide camera fitted with a quad-pixel sensor that adapts to the image being taken. The devices can record at a full 48 MP with ProRAW, which allows the capture of professional images.

The TrueDepth front-facing camera now has an enhanced f/1.9 aperture for improved selfies and video shooting in a dark environment, and it has now included autofocus for the first time.

Apple has designed the Adaptive True Tone flash with a series of 9 LEDs that adjust patterns depending on the lens focal length. Other photographic features include Photographic Styles, Smart HDR 4, Portrait Mode, Night Mode, etc.

It offers four storage options: 128GB, 256GB, 512GB, and 1TB storage capacities. Both devices also support Wi-Fi 6 and Bluetooth 5.3.

The Pro models also support 5G connectivity, Massif charging up to 15W, and fast charging through Lightning with a 20W or higher charger.

Parts of the iPhone 14

To begin our journey, let's learn a few things about the parts of your new iPhone. The diagram below highlights the important parts you need to know.

Buttons: The iPhone has three important buttons, the Side button, and two volume buttons. The Side button is used to turn off your iPhone and lock and unlock it. The volume buttons are used to increase and decrease your iPhone's volume.

Ring/Silent Switch: This switch is used for rapidly muting (and unmuting) your phone. Simply push it backward to mute and forward to unmute the phone (for example, when you're in a meeting).

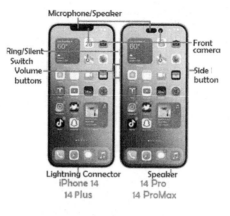

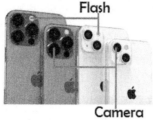

Cameras: There are two groups of cameras in the iPhone 14. One front camera for video calls and selfies, and two/three rear cameras for snapping photos of others, recording videos, scanning documents, and much other cool stuff. The rear cameras differ in their particular focal lengths and, as such, are given different names: Wide, Ultra Wide, and Telephoto.

Flash: You'll likely recognize the flash the very minute you see it. You can use it like a torch for illuminating your path while walking at night or searching for something in the dark. But far beyond this, you can use the flash to enhance the brightness and exposure of your pictures.

Microphone

Port: If you check the bottom of your phone, you'll see a port/hole. It's called a Lightning connector. It is where you'll insert your USB charger when you want to charge your phone or connect it to another device so that you can transfer data.

Note: There isn't any SIM tray, so you'll not have to worry about inserting a physical SIM card. Your iPhone uses an eSIM.

Accessories for your iPhone

What Comes In the Box

The iPhone currently comes with the following accessories:

Lightning-USB cable: For connecting to a computer and an AC adapter.

USB power adapter: For charging the battery. The size and type of adapter depend on the country or region.

You can also use the charging cable to connect your iPhone to your computer to download and transfer files, use your iPhone as a second screen on your Mac, and more. A picture of these two is shown below.

What You'll Need to Buy

The following accessories can easily be obtained from Amazon or other electronics shops. Although you can use your phone without getting them, your user experience will improve if you have them. Also, you'll be able to use your phone for a longer time without spending money to repair it or get another one.

Phone Case: For some people, a phone case is a must. Phones can sometimes be slippery. With a protective case, your phone will be able to survive even if you accidentally drop it without getting damaged. Various types are available (Silicone cases, leather, etc.), and they are quite affordable.

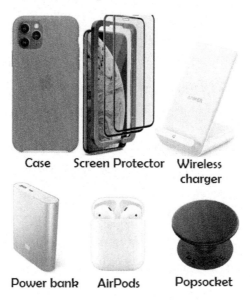

Case   Screen Protector   Wireless charger

Power bank   AirPods   Popsocket

Screen Protector: This is another accessory you should endeavor to get. Although you may not see the need immediately, you will over time. A screen protector/guard can prevent your phone's screen from scratching by keys and other sharp objects. But more importantly, they can prevent the cracking of the phone screen if you drop it, which will be a disaster if it happens.

Wireless Charger: For those who don't like having a lot of cords and wires around, you can get a Wireless charger for your phone. Some phone cases (batteries) have inbuilt wireless chargers, so try to do some searching (you'll save money and get more done).

Headphones: The most popular headphones for iPhones are the Apple AirPods. They don't have troublesome wires and connect to your iPhone superfast. Enjoy listening to songs, making phone calls on the go, and doing other crazy stuff.

Battery Pack (or Power Bank): There are various brands in the market (e.g., CONXWAN, Attom Tech, etc.) Although these are optional, they are very useful, especially if you are going on a business trip or traveling or live in an area with a poor power supply. A power bank is used for storing power that you can use to charge your phone whenever you need it. Many of them can juice up your battery multiple times (sometimes up to 8). Due to their small sizes, you can easily carry them around stress-free.

PopSockets: These are some ridiculously popular accessories among iPhone users. They are used for holding your iPhone in one hand while you take photos, browse the internet, and more. You could also use them as a stand for your phone. Due to their popularity, you may already have one. If you don't, know you'll be making a good investment if you get one.

CHAPTER 1: TERMINOLOGY

Control Center: Control Center is a feature of the iOS operating system that allows iOS devices to quickly access critical device settings by swiping up from the bottom of the screen. It's your one-stop shop for instant access to dozens of iPhone controls, including media playback, brightness, volume controls, mobile connectivity, screen mirroring, and so on. This quick-access menu lets you quickly access some of your iPhone's most frequently used and/or useful features and settings without launching the individual applications.

Airplane Mode: The iPhone and most mobile devices have airplane mode. When this feature is enabled, all wireless signals from your smartphone are blocked. An airplane icon will appear in the status bar at the top of your iPhone. Airplane mode disables cellular, Wi-Fi, and Bluetooth connectivity.

Cellular Data: To connect you to the internet, cellular data use the same network infrastructure used for cellphone calls, made available by cellphone towers. Unlike Wi-Fi, cellular data is always available if you're within your mobile service provider's coverage area.

Wi-Fi: This is the control for turning on your iPhone's Wi-Fi connectivity. A Wi-Fi network is essentially an internet connection distributed to various electronic devices such as computers, tablets, smartphones, and so on by a wireless router. It allows these devices to communicate with the internet via a wireless router.

Media Playback: This control allows you to manage media

files that are currently playing. You can pause or play a running media file from this panel or skip to the next song.

Portrait Orientation Lock: This feature prevents your iPhone's display from switching from portrait to landscape mode when tilted beyond a certain angle.

Do Not Disturb: This feature mutes your iPhone, allowing you to ignore calls and other notifications while you attend a meeting, eat, sleep, or work quietly. Your iPhone receives and stores all calls, messages, and notifications when in silent mode. Please do not disturb me.

Brightness Slider: The Brightness Slider allows you to manually control the brightness of your iPhone's screen. When you force-touch the brightness slider, you can also turn on or off True Tone, which automatically adjusts the brightness of your display based on the ambient lighting conditions in your immediate surroundings. Just beside the True Tone control switch is a Night Shift control, which allows you to manage the amount of blue light emitted by your iPhone's display.

Volume Slider: The volume control, or slider, on the control panel allows you to adjust your device's volume without pressing the volume rocker on the left side of the iPhone display. When you receive notifications, your device makes no noise, and its display does not light up, but you can still view them by physically turning on the display.

Screen Mirroring: Screen Mirroring is a wireless method of simultaneously reproducing what appears on one device's screen on another device's screen.

The flashlight feature on your iPhone can be accessed via the control center. Your iPhone's camera flash also functions as a flashlight, which is a useful tool for improving vision in low-light situations. It is powered by the flash mechanism built into the primary camera unit on the back of your iPhone, and it is located near the camera's lens.

Timer: The clock application's Timer can count down from a specific time to zero.

After you've set the timer, you can use other applications or even push the Sleep button, to put the iPhone in *Sleep Mode*. In the background, the timer will keep counting down, giving off a sound when the countdown is complete.

Calculator: The calculator application on your iPhone is a simple four-function calculating software for adding, subtracting, multiplying, and dividing. It can also function as a scientific calculator that can perform trigonometric and logarithmic calculations.

Camera: Tapping the camera icon takes you directly to the camera app.

Depending on your preference, other controls can be added to the control center.

CHAPTER 2: DIFFERENCES BETWEEN IOS 15 AND IOS 16

From a software perspective, the iPhone 13 come with iOS 15 pre-installed. The iPhone 12 models now work with iOS 14 but will be able to receive the update to iOS 15 next September 20.

iOS 16 comes standard on the iPhone 14 and iPhone 14 Plus. This update brings a redesigned Lock Screen and new communication, sharing, and intelligence features that revolutionize the iPhone user experience. With a layering effect that artistically places picture subjects in front of the clock and newly designed widgets that provide information at a glance, the Lock Screen is now more personalized, aesthetically pleasing, and useful than ever.

While it was widely predicted that Apple would drop support for the iPhone 6s with iOS 16 — a logical choice considering that it was released in 2015 — the company went much further with its official statement, cutting support for considerably more than the iPhone 6s.

According to Mark Gierman, the iOS 16 software will not be coming with entirely new updates over the iOS 15 software version in the meantime. But we have some new features added already on the iOS 16 software version powering the iPhone 14 device, such as a new overlook lock screen with more customizable ability; the imessages application is now going to support editing messages, deleting messages, and also marking them red

We also expect an iCloud share Photo Library feature with

friends and family and the capability to enable the percentage number we wish inside the battery icon.

The iOS 16 software version will support a dim dark background display to support the new Always-on-Display only on the iPhone 14 Pro-Models and won't be available on the iPhone 14 Standard versions.

CHAPTER 3: INTERNET AND APPS (HOW TO DOWNLOAD FILES, WI-FI, SAFARI, MAILS, IMESSAGE, ETC...)

Internet

Connect to a Wi-Fi Network

1. Navigate to Settings.

2. Tap the *Wi-Fi* menu.

3. From here, click the switch next to *Wi-Fi* to green.

4. Then, click on the name of the Wi-Fi you wish to join.

5. Input the Wi-Fi password if prompted.

Using Personal Hotspot

To do this, move to Settings and choose Personal Hotspot. Meanwhile, choose Cellular if you fail to find it on the main settings page. From that page, you will find the option to set it up, which also requires contacting your carrier. Once you enter your Hotspot settings, enable it and choose how you need to connect it to other devices.

How to Connect Via Bluetooth

To effectively use the Bluetooth option to share your internet connection, you must ensure the two devices have enabled their Bluetooth feature. Now, move to the Bluetooth settings on your device, check through, and choose the device you want to connect to. After the pairing process has been completed, the device you are attempting to connect will be able to browse web pages on the internet.

NB: To know if a device is sharing an internet connection with another device, simply check the status bar on your iPhone 13 and see that it has turned blue.

How to Connect Via USB

With the USB cable that arrived alongside your new device, you can proceed to connect to your PC or Mac and share your internet connection with other devices. Simply open the network preferences on your PC or Mac and choose your device from the available list.

Notwithstanding your chosen option to connect and share your internet connection with other devices, ensure you reduce how you open applications on your PC or Mac. This action will save you from spending more money on data, but you can freely use data on your PC and Mac if you subscribe to an unlimited plan.

How to Set Up Personal Hotspot

Setting up your hotspot and sharing it with others around you guarantees you are sharing your internet connection with them. This method works when the other individual enables their Wi-Fi and connects to your device when you also enable your hotspot.

1. Set up your hotspot in the following ways:

2. Open Settings and choose Personal Hotspot.

3. Touch the slider close to "Allow Others to Join."

4. Then, adhere to the steps to create your hotspot password. (*NB:* The personal hotspot password and name are what other devices require before they will be allowed to connect and use your hotspot).

Change or set your Wi-Fi password:

1. To do this, open Settings.

2. Move down until you locate your Personal Hotspot.

Turn On Mobile Data

1. Navigate to Settings.

2. Click *Cellular*.

3. From here, click the switch next to *Cellular Data* to green.

Enable Smart Data Mode

If you don't need 5G data all the time, switching on Smart Data can conserve battery life and reduce your data consumption. Want to enable Smart Data? Here's how:

1. Navigate to Settings.

2. Now, tap "*Cellular*" to see the options menu.

3. From here, tap *"Cellular Data Options."*

4. At this point, tap "*Voice & Data.*"

5. Finally, select "*5G Auto*" to turn on Smart Data mode.

App Management

The home screen contains an icon for each application on your device. It can be quite cluttered, especially if many apps are installed in the App Store. Here are some tips to customize your home screen so you can easily find your favorite apps anytime.

Rearrange your app icons: Press and hold the application on the home screen to reorder the icons. When the icon starts to shake, drag and drop it wherever you like. To move the icon to another screen, drag the icon to the left or right edge and press and hold until you switch to a new screen. You can move the application to and from the docking station if desired. When you're done, swipe upward from the base of the screen to stop the icon from shaking. If you're on the last page of your app, you can drag the icon to the far right to create an additional home screen. Once you finish, swipe upward from the bottom edge of your phone's screen.

Create a new folder: Drag one icon onto another to create a folder. Continue dragging and dropping the required icons to add them to the folder. It is a great way to organize similar applications and eliminate clutter from your home screen. Once you finish, swipe upward from the bottom of the screen.

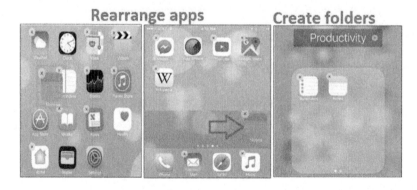
Rearrange apps   Create folders

Look for apps: Swipe down from the center of the home screen to search for apps. A search box is going to pop up at the up of the screen. When you start typing the name of the app you want, all apps that match your search will be displayed (along with other iPhone files and settings).

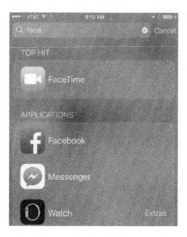

Delete apps: Press and hold the app on the home screen, then tap the *X* in the upper left corner to remove the app. Please note that embedded applications cannot be deleted. Once you finish, swipe up to go back to the home screen.

Open the App on the iPhone

You can quickly open the App from the main screen page or "App Database."

1. To go to the home screen, swipe up from the bottom edge of the screen. An illustration shows that you should go to the home screen by swiping up from the bottom.

2. An illustration will show that you should Swipe left to browse the App on other main screen pages.

3. Swipe left across all the main screen pages to view the "App Database," where your apps will be sorted.

4. To open the app, click on the image.

5. Go back to "App Database" by swiping up from the bottom screen.

Find and Open Apps in the "App Database"

1. Go to the home screen, and swipe left across all your home screen pages to go to the "App Database."

2. Click on the search field at the bottom of the top screen, and then input the name of the app you are looking for. Or scroll up and down to browse the alphabetical list.

3. To open the app, click it.

4. If the category has multiple small App images, you can click on them to expand the category and view all the apps in it.

Show and Hide the Main Screen Page

1. Press and hold the main screen until the App starts to swing.

2. Click on the dot at the bottom screen.

3. To hide the page, click to remove the tick.

4. To show the hidden pages, please click to add a tick.

5. Double-click "Finish" (on Face ID-equipped iPhones) or double-click the home button (on other iPhone models).

Arrange the Main Screen Pages

1. Press and hold the background of the main screen until the App starts to wiggle.

2. Click on the dot at the bottom screen.

3. To move each home screen page, long-press the page and drag it to a new location.

4. Double-click "Finish" on your device.

Change the Location to Download New Apps

1. Locate "Settings" > "Home Screen."

2. Select the option to place the new app on the main screen and the "App Database," or just to "App Database."

Move the App from the "App Database" to the Main Screen

1. You can add an app from the "App Database" to the main screen.

2. Long-press the App, and click "Add to Home Screen" (only available when the App is not on the home screen).

3. The app will be displayed on the main screen and "App Database."

App Store

There are hundreds of thousands of apps that you can access via the app store. You'll find everything from games to entertainment, productivity tools, and even applications that help you with your usual tasks, such as studying for exams, cooking dinner, and tracking travel plans.

There are thousands of apps that you can download for free. Many other applications cost as much as $ 0.99, but some are more expensive. To help you start your journey in the app store, you will find recommendations from the Store on things that are popular among users of iPhones.

The important features of the app store include the Account menu and 5 Tabs (Today, Games, Apps, Updates, and Search).

The first time you visit the App Store, you'll see a variety of new apps and games you can browse. If you're looking for something specific, you can press the App tab to move to the desired category.

Within each category, you will see a list of popular applications. Each app records its price (or tells you if it's free). You can check the details just by tapping the app. The app page contains info about the app's functions, user reviews, screenshots, and more.

You may need to run multiple programs on your computer simultaneously. It is also known as multitasking. Multitasking works a little differently on the iPhone. You can't use multiple apps simultaneously, but you can easily switch between apps without accessing the home screen. For example, you can navigate with Safari and choose to send a message through the mail application.

To make multitasking as easy as possible, the iPhone keeps recently interrupted apps in the background. If you move to a recent app, you don't have to wait for the app to load. Simply proceed from the point you paused.

Switching Between Apps

Swipe upward from the base of the screen till you get to the center of the screen, and then without letting go, hold the screen till the App switcher appears. A preview of the current application is displayed. You can swipe left or right to move between current applications. Just click the application to open it.

To close the app:

Switching to the home screen does not close the application you are using. It remains interrupted in the background. However, if the application does not work properly, it may be useful to force the application to close. It is similar to forcibly shutting down a program that does not respond on your computer.

Note that you don't need to close the app this way unless you have a problem. The app will be paused so your iPhone won't be slow, and its battery will not get drained.

Swipe upward from the base of the screen till you get to the center of the screen, and then without letting go, hold the screen till the App switcher appears. A preview of the current application is displayed. To close that application, simply slide upward on it. You can then start the application again from the home page.

Use App Switcher

1. To view all open apps in the "App Switcher," please use any of these:

2. Swipe up from the bottom of the screen and pause in the middle.

3. Swipe right to open the apps and click on the application you wish to use.

4. Exit and reopen the app on the iPhone

5. To exit the application, activate "App Switcher," swipe right to locate the app, and swipe up on the selected app.

6. To reopen the application, locate the main screen (or "App Database") and then tap the app.

How to Download Apps and Games

1. Tap on the app or game you searched for (it could be free, or you'll need to purchase it).

2. If it is free, tap on Get it or tap on the price if it is paid.

3. Next, activate Touch ID by Double-clicking the Face ID's side button or placing your finger on the Home button.

4. Apps installed from the App Store either appear on your Home screen or a subsequent screen of apps. First, you need to search for cool apps to get them: Head to the App Store and tap on the magnifying glass at the bottom of your screen (the search button).

5. Type in the app you want to search for and tap the search button.

Move Home Screen Apps

1. First, press and hold any icon.

2. Then, a thumbprint will be displayed on the upper left of the icon, and it will move like a wave.

3. The icon can now be moved.

4. Then press the icon you want to move with your finger.

5. Move your finger to the place you want to move without releasing your finger.

By the way, you can't place app icons anywhere on your iPhone, like Android smartphones.

There may be cases where you can use unofficial app icons, but app icons are arranged in order from the top.

Moving Apps to another Page

1. Long press the app

2. A thumbprint appears on all icons

3. Keep pressing the icon you want to move with your finger

4. Move to the page you want to move

5. Switch to the page you want to move and place an icon.

Create a Folder on the Home Screen

1. First, press and hold the icon.

2. To delete, move, or create a folder, you must first press and hold the icon; the thumbprint is displayed, and the icon is wavy.

3. You can now edit the home screen icons.

4. First, tap the icons you want to organize into a folder.

5. Then, a folder is automatically created.

6. Move and place the icon in the folder as it is.

How to Close Apps

1. Head to the app and hold the long line at the end of your screen with a finger.

2. Slide the line upwards to close the app.

How to Close multiple Apps

1. Open your home screen and slide the screen upwards from the bottom with your fingers.

2. You will see all the apps you open running in the background.

3. Slide each app upwards to close them.

How to Find an App

To find an application, use the search tab at the lower part of your screen. You can also search through categories like games, books, applications, and more if you do not know what you are looking for. To ease some stress, you can use Siri voice control to do your search. Just hold the Home button till Siri beeps.

How to Buy, Redeem, and Download an App

When you click on an application, you will be asked to either download it for free or make a payment. If the application is paid, know that you will purchase with your Apple ID's payment details. However, if the app displays what looks like a cloud, you have previously installed the app. Hence, you can install it again for free.

App Store Settings

1. You can set up your app store with different options by going to *Settings* and then to *iTunes & App Store*. It allows you to view and edit your account.

2. Change your Apple ID password.

3. Sign in with a new or different Apple ID.

4. Subscribe and turn on iTunes Match.

5. Turn on automatic downloads for books, music, tv, shows, movies, and more.

Control Offload Unused Apps

Remove unused apps on your device to free up storage space. In addition to automatically removing apps when the remaining storage capacity is low, you can also remove any apps manually.

By selecting "*iTunes Store & App Store*" from "*Settings*" on your iPhone and turning on "*Offload Unused Apps*," apps that are not in use are automatically used when the iPhone storage capacity is low and will be removed.

Commonly Used Apps

iMessage

Set a Name and Photo for Your iMessage Profile. Follow the steps below to add your name and picture to your Messaging app.

1. Launch the *Messages* app.

2. Tap at the top right side of your screen.

3. Select *Edit Name and Photo.*

4. Then select *Choose Name and Photo* on the next screen.

5. Input your first and last name, tap View More, and choose the photo you want to use for your profile.

6. Click *Edit* to choose a picture from your album. Alternatively, select an Animoji from the Animojis displayed.

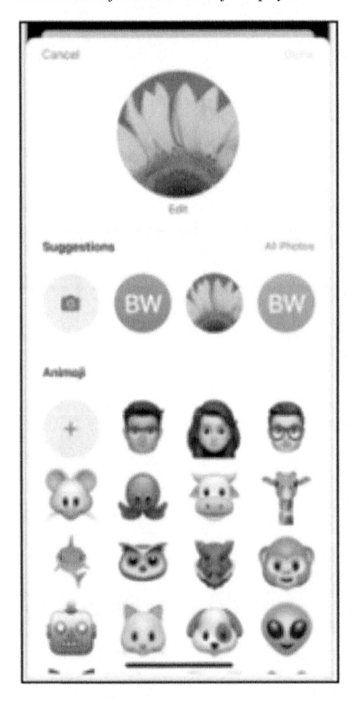

If you click on an Animoji, you would be asked on the next screen to *Select A Pose*.

1. Choose the pose that appeals to you.

2. Tap *Next* to get to the *Select a Color* screen.

3. Choose the color that you like.

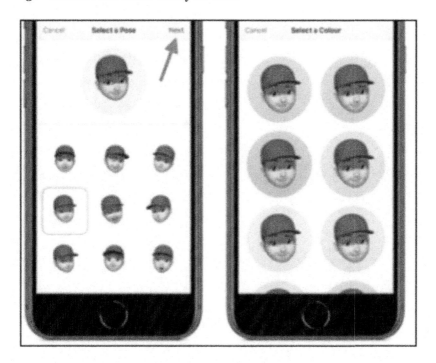

4. Tap *Done,* and you will be returned to the Profile name screen.

5. Tap *Continue.*

6. Tap *Use* if you want to use the picture for both Apple ID and your Contacts. Otherwise, tap *Not Now.*

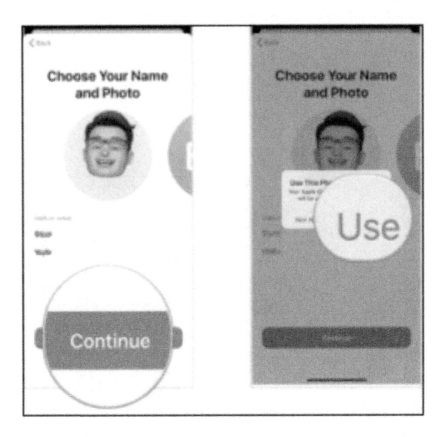

7. Tap *Continue.*

8. Select who should be able to view your name and picture. Tap *Contacts Only* if you want to grant access to all your contacts, or tap *Always Ask* if you want to select each time you send a message manually.

9. Tap *Done.*

Change Your Profile Photo Launch the *Messages* app.

1. Tap  at the top right side of your screen.

2. *Select* Edit Name and Photo.

1. Tap *Edit*.

2. *Tap* All Photos.

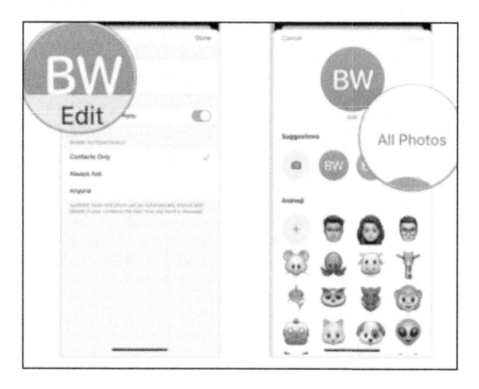

3. Click on the picture you want to use.

4. Fit the picture into the circle.

5. Add your filter.

6. Tap *Done*.

Select Your Initials As Your Profile Picture. Follow the steps below to use your name initials as your profile picture:

1. Launch the *Messages* app.

2. Tap ••• at the top right side of your screen.

3. *Select* Edit Name and Photo.

4. Tap *Edit*.

5. On the next screen, under Suggestions, you will find an image that contains your initials. Select the one that you like.

6. Choose your preferred color On the following screen.

7. Tap *Done*.

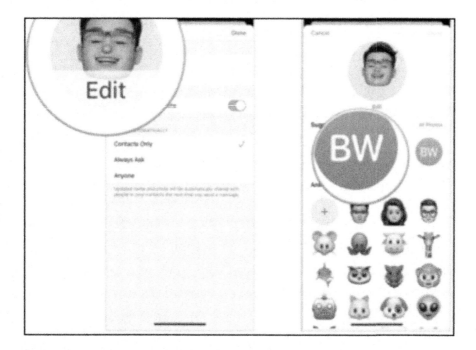

Edit a Sent iMessage

You can edit a message you've already sent. However, once it's past fifteen minutes, you'll be unable to do this.

1. Head to the Messages app.

2. Navigate to the conversation thread with the sent message you intend to edit.

3. Long-press the sent message you intend to edit.

4. Press "*Edit*" from the pop-up menu.

5. Go ahead with the changes and press the blue tick to confirm.

Report Junk SMS & MMS Messages

Messages from unknown senders can be reported as junk.

1. Head to the message and press the blue Report Junk button that shows up under it.

2. After this, press "***Delete and Report Junk***" to confirm.

Disable Read Receipts in iMessage

The way we send and receive text messages has improved thanks to instant messaging systems. They're quick, and you don't need a data plan to use them; you can quickly share media and more. However, many individuals find the Read Receipts feature to be extremely annoying.

The "**Read Receipt**" will force you to respond immediately, regardless of whether or not you actually want to. You know you're asking for problems if you wait to respond to a message, as the recipient can see when you've read it, and some people will inevitably find a way to create an issue out of it. You can easily turn off read receipts in the iMessage app's settings. Here's how:

1. Head to the Settings app.

2. Move down and press "***Messages***."

3. Move down and toggle off "***Send Read Receipts***."

4. That's it!

Sending Messages

1. Set up your Device for iMessaging from the Settings app. Go to *Messages*.

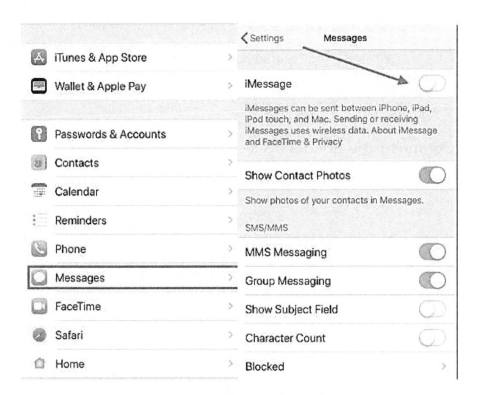

2. Enable *iMessages* by moving the slider to the right.

Set up Your Device for MMS

1. From *Settings*, go to *Messages*.

2. Enable *MMS Messaging* by moving the slider to the right.

Compose and Send iMessage

1. Click on the New Message option at the top right of the screen from the Message icon.

2. Under the "*To*" field, type in the first few letters of the receiver's name.

3. Select the receiver from the drop-down.

4. You will see iMessage in the composition box only if the receiver can receive iMessage.

5. Click on the *Text Input Field* and type in your message.

6. Click on the send button beside the composed message.

7. Your iMessage can send video clips, pictures, audio, and other effects.

Compose and Send SMS

1. Click on the New Message option at the top right of the screen from the Message icon.

2. Under the "*To*" field, type in the first few letters of the receiver's name.

3. Select the receiver from the drop-down.

4. Click on the "*Text Input Field*" and type in your message.

5. Click on the send button beside the composed message.

Compose and Send SMS With Pictures

1. Click on the New Message option at the top right of the screen from the Message icon.

2. Under the "*To*" field, type in the first few letters of the receiver's name.

3. Select the receiver from the drop-down.

4. Click on the *Text Input Field* and type in your message.

5. Click the *Camera* icon on the left side of the composed message.

6. From *Photos*, go to the right folder.

7. Select the picture you want to send.

8. Click *Choose* and then *Send*.

Create New Contacts

1. From Messages on iPhone, go to the Messages app.

2. Click on the conversation with the sender whose contact you want to add.

3. Click on the sender's phone number at the top of the screen, then click on *Info*.

4. On the next screen, click on *the arrow* by the top right side of your screen.

5. Then click *Create New Contact*.

6. Input their name and other details you have on them.

7. At the top right-hand of the screen, click on *Done*.

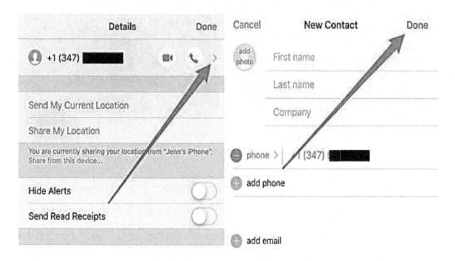

Hide Alerts in the Message App on Your iPhone

1. Go to the *Message app* on your iPhone.

2. Open the conversation you wish to hide the alert.

3. Click on ⓘ at the upper right corner of the page.

4. Among the options, one of them is *Hide alerts*; move the switch to the right to turn on the option (the switch becomes green).

5. Select *Done* at the upper right corner of your screen.

Safari

Safari is a browser built into the iPhone. It's similar to other browsers like Google Chrome or Internet Explorer. Use this to access the webpage on your device. Safari's interface is similar to that found in desktop browsers, and it also has some unique features that make mobile browsers easier.

View and Reopen Recently Closed Tabs in Safari

1. Open the *Safari* app.

2. Click on the ⬜ button at the bottom right side of your screen.

3. Tap and hold the new tab⊕ button until you see a list of the Recently Closed Tabs.

4. Click on a site to open the address in a new tab.

5. Tap *Done* to exit.

Recently Closed Tabs	Done
Wikipedia wikipedia.org	

Customize Your Favorite Site in Safari

1. On the Safari home page, you will find recommended, favorite, and frequently visited sites and Siri suggestions. This guide will show you how to customize your favorite websites.

2. On the homepage of the Safari browser, under the *Favorites* section, click and hold a website's favicon to display the preview screen and the contextual menu. There are a couple of other options, including *Edit* and *Delete*.

3. Tap *Edit* to rename the site as you want it to show on your Favorites.

4. In the website address field, you can also enter a different website to take you to a different part of that site.

Bookmark Multiple Open Tabs in Safari

Follow the steps below to bookmark different websites at once:

1. Open all the sites you plan to bookmark.

2. Let one of the websites be in the main browsing window.

3. Press long on  at the bottom of your screen.

4. Click on *Add Bookmarks for X Tabs* on the next screen.

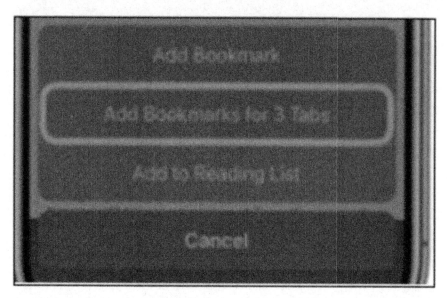

5. On the next screen, save the tabs in a new bookmark folder, choose from the current list, and click *Save* at the top of the page to save your bookmarks.

Close All Your Open Tabs at Once

Follow the steps below to close all your open tabs at the same time:

- Method 1

    1. Open the *Safari* browser.

    2. Press long on 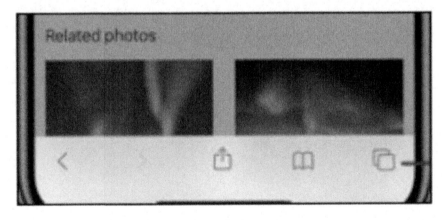 at the right side of the bookmark icon.

3. Select *Close All Tabs*.

· Method 2

1. Tap once on  icon to display the Window view.

2. Press long on *Done*.

3. Select *Close All Tabs*.

Automatically Close Safari Tabs

Set up your browser to close open tabs at a defined time.

1. Tap *Safari* in the *Settings* app.

2. Select *Close Tabs*.

3. Select your preferred option on the next screen.

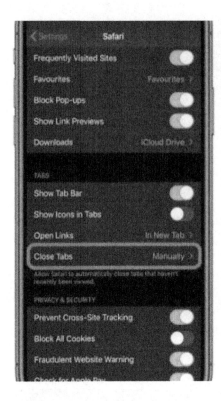

Safari Share Sheet

Follow the steps below to share a web page as a link, archive, or PDF file:

1. Open the website you want to share.

2. Tap ⬆️ to display the Share Sheet.

3. Click your sharing method from the list. Tap *More* to see other options.

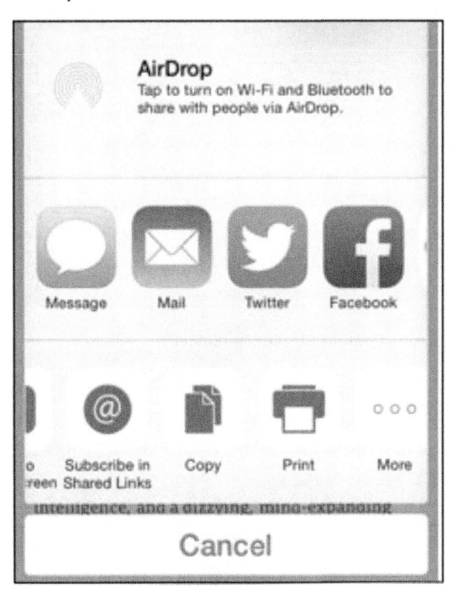

4. Select your sharing method and tap *Options* to choose to send as an archive, link, or PDF.

Enable Content Blockers in Safari

Content blockers offer a one-trick solution for prohibiting ads like popups and banners from stacking on websites you visit. They can shield you from online tracking by deactivating cookies and scripts that sites try to load.

1. Open the *Settings* app.

2. Next, press *Safari*.

3. Under *General*, touch *Content Blockers*.

4. To activate content blockers, flip the switches to the ON position.

Note: the Content Blockers option doesn't appear in Safari's settings until you've installed a third-party content blocker from the App Store.

Temporarily Disable Content Blockers in Safari

1. Open Safari on your iPhone and go to the site in question.

2. Next, press the "aA" icon in the upper left corner of the screen to uncover the *Website View* menu.

3. Press *Turn Off Content Blockers*.

If you only need to disable content blockers for a particular website, tap *Website Settings* in the *Website View* menu, and afterward, flip the switch next to *Use Content Blockers* to the OFF position.

Mail App

Mail is likely one of the first apps you want to set up on your iPhone. You can use it to view and send emails, reply to messages, and manage your inbox. It is all you normally do with your email account.

The first time you open an email, you must sign in to your existing email address. Select your email provider and follow the instructions to connect your account to your email application. Once complete, you can send and receive emails from that account on your iPhone.

Add another Email Account

If you use multiple email accounts (for example, one for personal email and one for business email), you can add multiple accounts to your email application. It allows you to manage all your messages in one place.

To add another email account, open Settings on the home

screen and go to *Password & Accounts> Add Account.* Simply follow the directions that pop up to sign in with your new account.

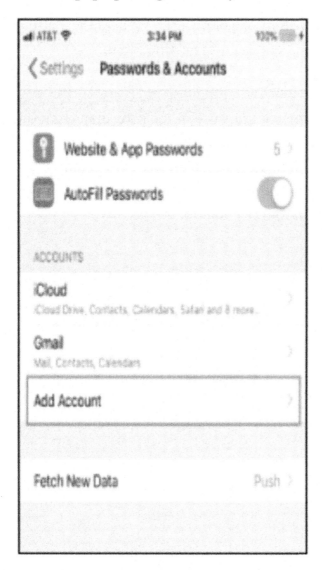

Email Notification

A badge will appear on the application icon when you receive a new email. This number shows the number of unread emails in your inbox. It allows you to quickly check for new messages without opening the mail application.

You can customize your alerts by opening Settings, tapping Notification Center, and selecting Email.

Slide GESTURE

The Mail app contains useful tools for managing your inboxes, such as folders and flags. Swipes can also be used to manage messages in the mail inbox quickly. For example, you can slide a message to the left if you wish to archive or delete it, reply to it, and forward it or something else.

Personalize Your Email Signature

By default, every email you send contains the word "sent from iPhone" at the bottom of the message. It is the default email signature for your email application. If you want to customize or delete your email signature, open Settings from your home screen, tap Email, then scroll down and select Signature.

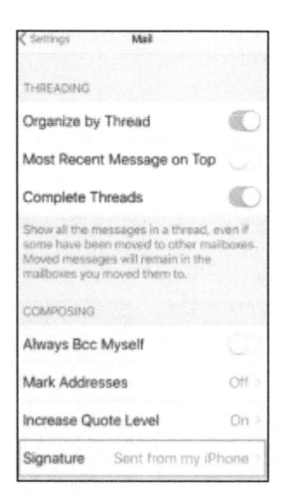

Apple Maps

Apple updated their Maps app to include features such as sharing estimated arrival time with other people, collections (allows you to create lists of local interesting spaces and spots), keeping track of special locations, and so much more. In this section, we will explore the features of Apple Maps.

Share Your ETA

When you share your ETA with family and friends, they can

view your estimated time of arrival on a trip or any changes that occur during that trip.

1. Launch the Apple *Maps*.

2. Search for your destination in the search bar, or select your destination from your *Favorite* or *Recently Viewed* to bring up an address fast.

3. Click on *Directions* to start your journey. Don't forget to select your means of transportation, whether *Walk, Ride, Drive,* or *Transit.*

4. Tap *Go* to begin your journey.

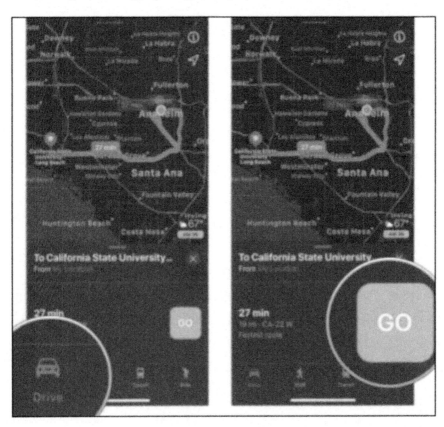

5. Navigate to the bottom of the screen and click on *Share ETA.*

6. Click on the contact you wish to share your movement with.

View Another Person's ETA

You will receive a notification on your phone whenever someone shares their ETA with you. You can view and get live updates on their trip.

1. Select the ETA notification to take you directly to Apple *Maps*.

2. You will see their journey and estimated arrival time on the map.

Stop Sharing ETA

Follow the steps below to stop sharing your ETA:

1. Open the *Maps* app, which still shows directions.

2. At the bottom of the screen, tap *Sharing ETA with X (number) people*.

3. Select the contact whom you no longer wish to share your ETA with.

4. Your phone will instantly stop sharing your ETA with that person.

Create Favorite Locations

If you frequent a place like your office address, you may Favorite the address to have the address always show at the top of the Maps screen. You can also view the estimated time of arrival for your favorited locations. Follow the steps below to add a location to your Favorite bar:

1. Launch the *Maps* app.

2. Pull up the search bar indent until the map is no longer showing (please refer to screenshot).

3. Go to the Favorite section and tap *Add*.

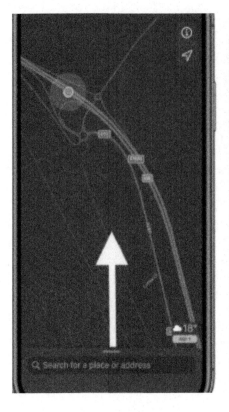

4. Type the address or name of the place you want to favorite. To search using your voice, tap the Siri icon and call out the name or address.

5. Look for the address under *Suggestions,* then tap the ⊕ icon to add that address to your Favorites.

6. On the next screen, tap *Label* if you wish to change the place's name.

7. Under *Type,* choose your preferred option that best describes the place.

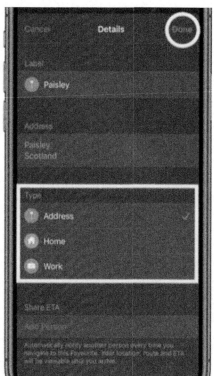

8. Click on *Add Person* under *Share ETA* to share your journey to this location with your contact.

9. Tap *Done* to complete the setup.

Delete Favorite

Follow the steps below to remove an address from your Favorites:

1. From the home screen of Apple *Maps*, tap *See All* (beside *Favorites*).

2. Click on the ![info icon] icon beside the saved location you want to delete.

3. Then select *Remove Favorite* at the bottom of your screen.

Create Collections in the Map

Create a collection of places in your desired destination to help you keep track of, even before you reach your destination. For instance, if you plan to visit Florida and want to take the kids to Disney World while there, you can create a Collection for Florida, then add all the places you would like to visit while in Florida. Follow the steps below to create a collection:

1. From the *Maps* home screen, drag the handle at the bottom to expand the panel.

2. From Collections, click on *New Collections*.

3. Choose a name for your Collection, then tap *Create.*

4. Your Collection is ready.

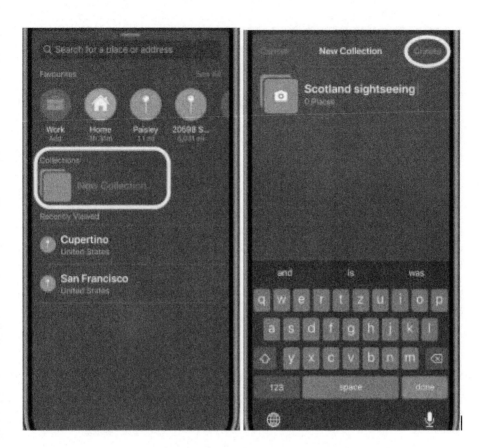

Add Addresses to Your Collections

Follow the steps below to add addresses to the Collections that you created:

1. Click on the new collection you just created.

2. Navigate to the bottom of your screen and tap *Add a Place*.

3. Type the address, place, or landmark you want to visit.

4. Click ⊕ beside the desired location under *Suggestions*. To add other addresses, clear the search bar, type the new address or place, and click ⊕ again beside the new address.

5. Tap *Done* once you finish adding all the places to your Collection.

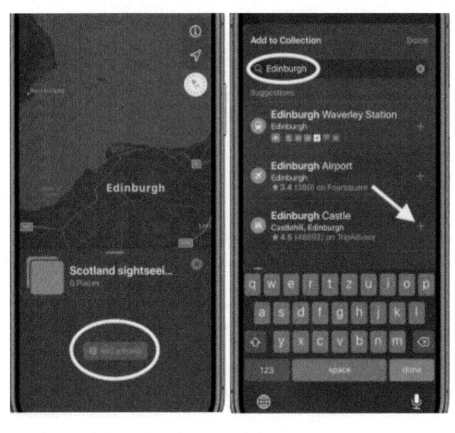

Delete an Address from Your Collections

To remove an address, place, or location from your collections, follow the steps below:

1. Launch the Apple *Maps*.

2. Tap a collection to open it.

3. Navigate to the bottom of your screen and click on *Edit*.

4. Select the addresses or places you want to delete.

5. Tap *Delete* to remove the addresses or locations from that Collection.

Explore Your Collection Locations

Click on the address to learn more about a location in your Collections.

1. Click on *Directions* to see how you can get to that location.

2. Tap *Flyover* to have a close look at the area.

3. To add a location to your Favorite, click on the location, scroll down, and tap *Add to Favorite*.

4. Click on *Report an Issue* if you find anything amiss about the location.

5. To add this location to another Collection, tap *Add* at the top of your screen.

6. Select *Share* to send the details of this location to family or friends via messaging apps.

Clock app

How to Set an Alarm

Among the more modest tweaks is a redesigned Clock app. The clock app on this device is simpler but also a bit counterintuitive in others.

How to use alarms Head to the Clock app and tap on the "Alarm tab."

Tap the plus "+" icon or hit Edit and tap on an existing alarm to modify it. Use the number keypad to enter your alarm time, or you can swipe up or down on the orange time to use it as a wheel picker.

Tap Save

You can also use Siri to set alarms or the Sleep Schedule feature. If you start by tapping the orange alarm time at the top, only the hour or minutes to be edited will be selected. However, you can use the number pad to enter your alarm time quickly.

Find My App

The Find My app on your iPhone can help you track down your missing Apple device or that of your loved ones, even if the phone goes off. It also lets you remotely erase the device's data, lock it with a password, and more. Apple's Find My service helps you track down your or your family member's lost or stolen device, remotely wipe the data, lock your phone, and more.

Turn On Find My

Make sure Find My iPhone is turned on, which is findable when missing.

1. Launch the Settings app.

2. Click on your profile banner at the top.

3. Click *Find My*.

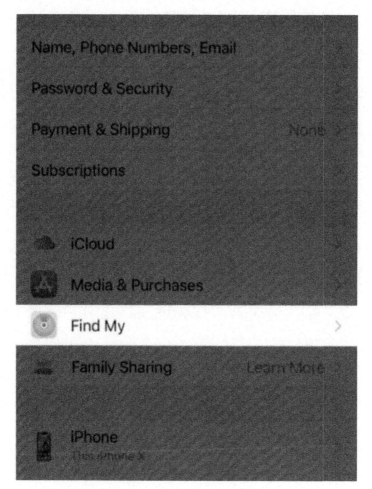

4. Next, click *Find My iPhone*.

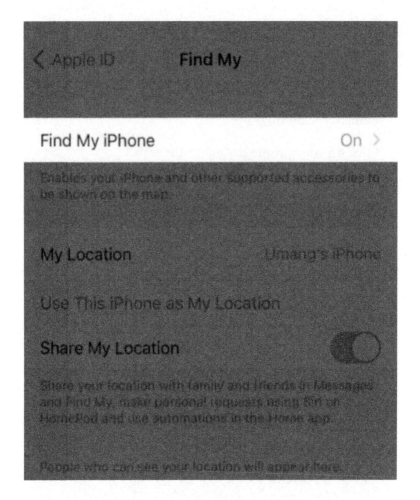

5. After that, click the **_Find My iPhone_** toggle to the ON position.

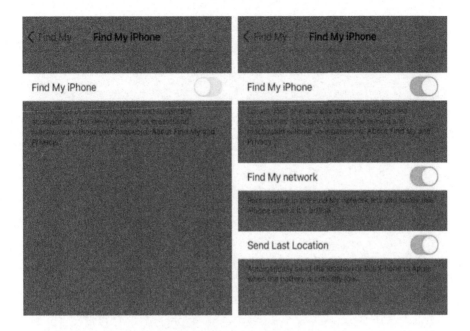

6. Turn on **Enable Offline Finding.**

7. Make sure **Send Last Location** is also turned on.

Use Find My App to Locate your Lost Device

As previously explained, if you lose your phone, you can use the Find My app to track it down and delete all of its data. You can set the phone to get map directions or report loss using the app. Nonetheless, before searching for your missing iPhone, ensure that Find My iPhone is turned on in Settings. If so, let's get started with the tracking process. It also applies to an iPad.

View the Lost Device on a Map

1. Launch the Find My app.

2. Look to the bottom and click on the **Devices** tab.

3. Click on the device to see its location on the map.

Note: You can also see the devices of a family-sharing group if you're a member.

4. Click on "**Directions**" to see that location on the Maps application.

5. If you already enabled **Offline Finding**, you can find the device even if it's not connected to a cellular data or Wi-Fi network.

Play a Sound

1. Launch the Find My app.

2. Click on the **Devices** tab.

3. After that, click on the missing device and click **Play Sound**.

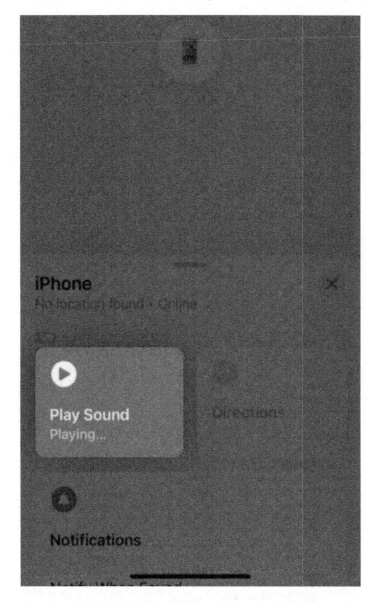

4. No sound will play if it's offline unless it is paired to an internet network.

Mark a Device as Lost Mode

1. Open the Find My app.

2. Click on the **Devices** tab.

3. After that, click on the missing device.

4. From there, scroll down and click **Mark as Lost**.

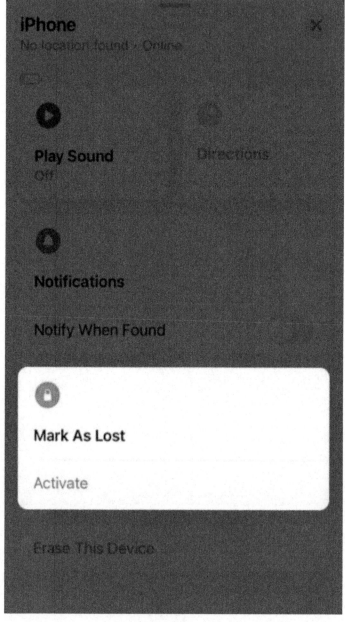

5. Next, click *Activate*.

6. Follow the onscreen prompt.

Erase the Lost Device Remotely

If you still can't find your iPhone after attempting the above steps, you should consider erasing the data on the device. Be sure you really want to do this because it can't be undone, and you can't locate it through the Find My app any longer.

1. Open the Find My app.

2. Click on the *Devices* tab.

3. After that, click on the device you want to wipe clean.

4. Then, scroll down and click on "*Erase This Device.*"

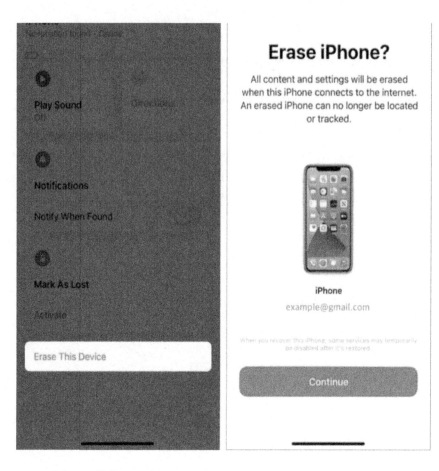

5. Next, click on **Continue**.

Locate your Friends with Find My App

The Find My app doesn't just help you locate your missing devices; it can also help you track down your friends and loved ones.

Siri

Ask Siri on iPhone

Talking to Siri allows you to complete your work quickly. Ask

Siri to translate words, set alarms, find locations, report weather conditions, and more.

The voice will be processed on the iPhone, but the transcription of your request will be sent to Apple to improve Siri. This data will not be associated with your Apple ID and will only be stored for a limited period. You can also share your recording files with Apple for improved purposes.

The notification of the "Clock" app shows that the 8:00 am alarm is turned on. The button at the bottom center of the screen can be used to continue the conversation with Siri.

Prepare Siri for action

In case you forgot to prepare Siri when you did the same for the device for the first time, locate "Settings" > "Siri and Search," and then do any of the following:

- To activate Siri by voice: Enable "Listen to "Hey Siri."

- To enable Siri using a button: Enable the "Press the side button to use Siri."

- To change Siri's settings, please refer to "Change Siri settings on iPhone."

Re-enable Siri with your voice

If you activate Siri by voice, it will read the response aloud. Please shout "Hey Siri," and then make Siri answer a question or request to perform an action for you.

For instance, say: "Hey Siri, what's the weather today?", "Hey Siri, the school alarm clock rings at eight o'clock in the morning."

If you want to ask Siri other questions or perform other tasks, please shout out "Hey Siri" again or ensure you Click the "Listen" button.

To prevent your device from replying to "Hey Siri," turn the device face down, or go to "Settings" > "Siri and Search," and then disable "Listen to "Hey Siri."

Enable Siri with the Button

If you enable Siri to use a button, she will respond quietly when the device is in silent mode. When silent mode is disabled, Siri will speak the response.

· Press and hold the side button.

When Siri is displayed, make Siri answer a question or ask to perform an action you want to be carried out. For instance: "How much is 225 times 18%?" or "Time for three minutes." To ask Siri questions or perform other tasks, Click the "Listen" button.

· If Siri misunderstands what you mean, please correct it.

· Put the request "Listen" button differently: click on it and then express the request in other ways.

· Spell out part of the request: Click once the "Listen" button and make your request known again by typing words that she doesn't understand. For instance, say "Dial" and string out the names of people in the address book.

· Modify the content before sending the message: talk about "change."

· Use text editing request: If your request pops up on the screen, you can modify it. Click on the request and utilize the on-screen keyboard.

- Use typing in place of talking for talking to Siri.

- Locate "Settings" > "Accessibility"> Siri, and enable "Enter to talk to Siri."

To request something, please enable Siri, and utilize the keyboard and text fields to pose Siri some questions or request actions for you.

Find out What Else Siri Can Do on iPhone

Use Siri on iPhone to get data and perform operations. Siri and its reply will be displayed above the operation you are performing so you can refer to the data on the screen.

Siri is interactive. When Siri displays a web link, you can click to view more information in your default web browser. Siri's replies on the screen contain buttons or controls; you can Click and continue the action. You can Click Siri again to ask another question or ask Siri to perform other tasks for you.

The following are examples of requests you can make to Siri. More examples are shown in this guide. You can also ask Siri: "Hey Siri, do you know how to do it?"

Use Siri to Answer Questions

Use Siri to find objective facts quickly, perform calculations, or translate words into other languages. For example:

- "Hey Siri, play the sound of rain."

- "Should I say" the Mandarin in a little bit?"

Siri translates the Cantonese phrase "Which" into Mandarin. The button on the right of the translation can replay the translated audio.

Use Siri with App

You can use Siri to control the App with your voice. For example:

- "Hey, Siri, make an appointment at nine o'clock in Dawen" to make the itinerary in "Calendar."

- "Hey, Siri, add onions to the shopping list" to add items to the "reminders."

- "Hey, Siri, what's my update?" (please speak in English) to get the weather, news, reminders, and calendar itinerary in your area.

- For more examples, check out any of the following items:

- Ask Siri to read calls, messages, and other items on iPhone

- Use Siri to play music on iPhone

- Use Siri to control your home on your iPhone

- Use Siri, "Map" and "Map" widgets to get directions on iPhone

- Add Siri shortcut on iPhone

Use Siri to Share Data with Contacts

You can share items such as pictures, home pages, and other web pages and locations with contacts in your address book.

For example, when looking for a photo in the "Photos" gallery, you can say, "Hey Siri, send this mommy" to create a new message using that photo.

The "Photos" app is open, and there is a photo of two people. There is a message addressed to "grannies" above the photo, which contains the same photo. Siri is at the bottom of the screen.

Use Siri to Personalize Your Experience

The more you use Siri, the more Siri understands your needs. You can also tell Siri about your personal information and change the way Siri responds.

Tell Siri about Your Personal Information on Your iPhone

You can provide Siri with information (including home and company addresses, as well as the relationship between relatives and friends) to get a more personalized experience, such as "show driving directions to the company back to the house" and "FaceTime grandma."

Tell Siri Your Identity

1. Open the "Contacts" and fill in your contact details.
2. Locate "Settings" > "Siri and Search"> "My Profile" and click on your name.

Tell Siri about your relatives and friends

For example, "Hey, Siri, Jiali is my wife," or "Hey, Siri, Jingyi is my grandmother."

Keep Siri Up to Date with What You Know Between Apple Gadgets

On your gadget, locate "Settings" and log in with the same Apple ID.

If you use iCloud, the system will use end-to-end encryption to keep your Siri settings up-to-date on your Apple device.

If you don't want Siri personalized content to be updated

between your iPhone and your other devices, you can disable Siri in the iCloud settings.

1. Go to "Settings"> [your name]> iCloud, and turn off Siri.

Ask Siri to Read Calls, Messages, and Other Items on iPhone

On supported headsets and CarPlay, Siri can read incoming calls and notifications from apps such as "Messages." You can use your voice to answer or reply without saying, "Hey, Siri."

"Read out incoming calls" and "Read out notifications" can also be used in conjunction with supported third-party apps.

Ask Siri to Read out Incoming Calls

With "Read Out Calls," Siri will recognize incoming phone calls and FaceTime calls, allowing you to use voice to answer or reject calls.

1. Go to "Settings" > "Siri and Search"> "Read Calls," and select an option.

When you receive an incoming call, Siri will recognize the caller and ask if you want to answer the call. Please say "listen" to answer the call or "don't listen" to refuse to answer.

Tell Siri to Read Notifications

Siri can automatically read notifications from apps such as "Messages" and "Reminders." Siri will automatically enable App notifications for apps that use time-sensitive notifications, but you can change the settings anytime.

1. Go to "Settings" > "Siri and Search"> "Read Out Notifications" and turn on "Read Out Notifications."

2. Click the app you want Siri to read out notifications from that app, and then turn on "Read Out Notifications."

For apps that you can send a reply to (such as "message"), Siri will repeat what you have said and then ask for confirmation before sending a reply. If you want to send a reply without waiting for confirmation, please turn on "No confirmation when replying."

Add Siri Shortcut on iPhone

Some apps will provide you with shortcuts to manipulate content frequently. You can just use Siri to start these shortcuts. For example, the "Travel" app may allow you to view your upcoming itinerary by asking Siri, "Will I go on my next journey?"

Join the Suggested Shortcut

When you see the suggested shortcut, Click "Join Siri" and follow the on-screen instructions to record the words you chose to execute the shortcut.

You can also use the "Shortcuts" App to create shortcuts using Siri, or manage, re-record and delete existing Siri shortcuts. Please refer to Shortcut Manual.

Files App

Apple's iOS devices have a built-in file manager called the Files app. The app organizes your device storage. It works with other cloud storage services like Google Drive, Dropbox, and more. The Files app makes it easy to save and access your media files (such as music, images, PDFs, etc.) in one place. Here, you'll learn how to use the Files app.

Adding Third-party Apps

If you want to turn on third-party applications in the Files application, you will need to download the applications from the App Store. Afterward, follow these steps:

1. Navigate to the Files app.

2. Press "*Browse*."

3. Here, press the three dots icon at the upper right.

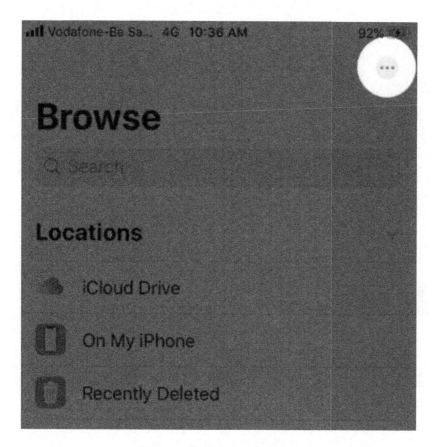

4. Then, press "***Edit***."

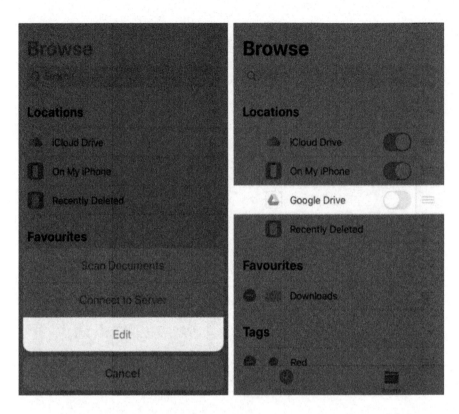

5. Turn on the toggle next to third-party apps such as Dropbox, Google Drive, and Adobe Creative Cloud.

6. Lastly, press "*Done.*"

Check Files Stored Locally

1. Navigate to the Files app.

2. Press "*Browse.*"

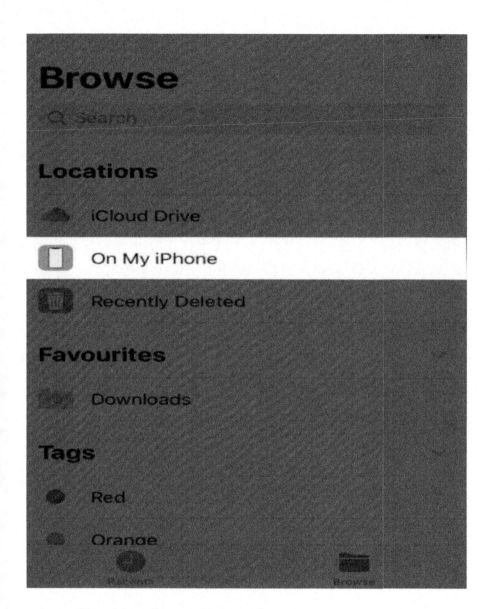

3. Here, press "*On My iPhone*."

4. In this place, you can view all the files saved locally on your phone. If the "*On My iPhone*" option doesn't appear, follow the above steps of adding third-party apps to turn it on.

Create New Folders

1. Underneath the "*iCloud Drive*" or "*On My iPhone*" option, long-press an empty portion.

2. Then, press "*New Folder.*"

3. Insert a name and press "*Done.*"

Search for Files

You'll notice a search field at the top when you're in the Files app. Click on it and type in the file's name to look for it. After this, the search result will show where the file is saved, such as iCloud Drive. Click on the file from the search result to see its content.

Adding a Favorite Folder

1. Navigate to the Files app.

2. Press "*Browse.*"

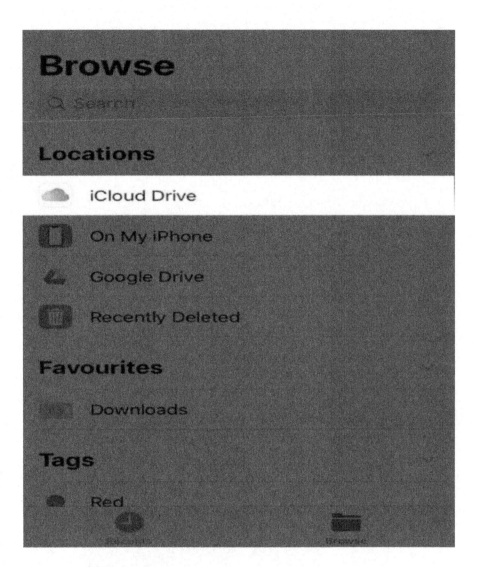

Browse

Q Search

Locations

☁ iCloud Drive

▢ On My iPhone

◢ Google Drive

🗑 Recently Deleted

Favourites

Downloads

Tags

● Red

3. Select a location.

4. Once you see a folder, press and hold it.

5. Then, click on *"Favorite."*

6. From there, press *"Browse"* from the lower row, and under *"Locations,"* you'll see the header labeled *"Favorites."* You'll see your favorite folder under it.

View Your Recently Accessed Files

1. Navigate to the Files app.

2. Press "*Recent*" from the lower row.

3. From here, you can now see all of the recently opened files.

Move Multiple Files

1. Navigate to the Files app.

2. Press the "*Browse*" tab.

3. Navigate to the location where you've saved the document.

4. Then, press "*Select*" at the top right.

5. Go ahead and choose multiple files.

6. Then, press on a single folder icon.

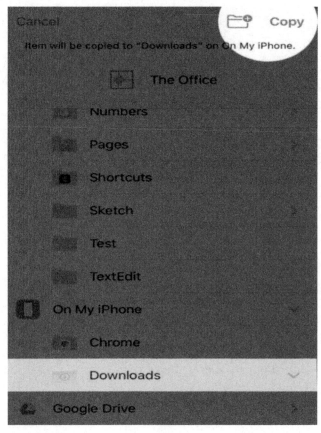

7. After this, choose a location and press *"Copy."*

Duplicate Multiple Docs

1. Navigate to the Files app.

2. Press the *"Browse"* tab.

3. Navigate to the location where you've saved the file.

4. Then, press *"Select"* at the top right.

5. Go ahead and choose multiple files.

6. Press the folder icon with a plus.

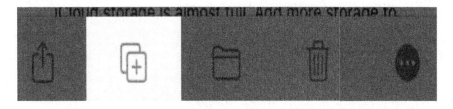

7. After this, duplicates of the chosen documents will be created. They'll have the word '2' attached as a suffix to the file name.

Share Docs & Folders

1. Navigate to the Files app.

2. Press the *"Browse"* tab.

3. Navigate to the location where you've saved the file.

4. Long-press on the document.

5. Click on *"Share"* and then choose to share via Email, AirDrop, third-party apps, etc.

Add Tags in Files App

1. Navigate to the Files app.

2. Press the *"Browse"* tab.

3. Navigate to the location.

4. Long-press the file and click on "*Tags*."

5. Go ahead and choose a color tag or "*Add New Tag*."

6. Then, press "*Done*."

7. Click on "*Browse*." In this place, you'll see a header titled "*Tags*." Click on a tag to view all the files under it.

Remove Files in File App

1. Navigate to the Files app.

2. Press the "*Browse*" tab.

3. Navigate to the location.

4. Long-press a file.

5. From the pop-up, press "*Delete*." After this, the file will be instantly deleted.

Delete Multiple Files

1. Navigate to the Files app.

2. Press the "*Browse*" tab.

3. Navigate to the location where you've multiple files.

4. Press "*Select*" from the top right. Follow up by choosing multiple files by tapping on their icons.

5. Click the delete icon at the lower row. After this, the multiple files will be removed.

Recover Deleted Files

If you mistakenly deleted a file, you can recover it. Here's how:

1. Navigate to the Files app.

2. Press the "*Browse*" tab.

3. Here, press "*Recently Deleted*" underneath the "*Locations*" header.

4. To recover just one file, long-press it and choose "*Recover.*" After this, the file will be instantly reinstated to its original location.

5. Suppose you wish to recover multiple deleted files in one go; press "*Select*" and choose the files. Lastly, press "*Recover.*"

Other iPhone 14 Apps

Calendar App

You can add calendar events to your iPhone using the Calendar app, and you will be notified when the event's date approaches. To add an event, open the Calendar app and tap the event day or the Plus sign below the battery indicator in the upper right corner of your display. The Apple Calendar app can also sync with your Google Calendar and settings to ensure that all of your events are accessible across many platforms.

Numbers App

Numbers is a spreadsheet program created specifically for iOS-enabled mobile devices. The program features Multi-Touch gestures and the Smart Zoom function, allowing you to create excellent spreadsheets with just your fingers. It is the second of three apps that comprise the iPhone's iWork productivity package.

Wallet App

The Wallet app keeps sensitive financial information, like

credit card information, so you can conveniently make online transactions without constantly pulling out your credit card.

Podcasts

Podcasts is Apple's podcast app, which is preloaded on iOS devices and allows you to listen to your favorite podcasts from around the world.

iMovie

On your iOS device, you may use the iMovie app, a video editing software tool, to create, edit, and export high-quality movies and trailers. The program can be used to change and improve the color configuration of videos and their playback speed and stabilize shaky images.

YouTube app

Although the YouTube app does not come preloaded on your iPhone, I urge that you download it because it is a wonderful resource for content-rich, instructive, and enlightening films.

iTunes

The iTunes app, which is Apple's client application for the iTunes Store, is an online music store, media player, and music library where registered users can purchase music using a credit card. It also features Internet radio channels where users may listen to the greatest Internet radio.

Stocks App

As the name suggests, the Stocks app allows you to monitor stock values in real-time. You may also look at the market capitalization of various stock exchanges worldwide, their gains and losses, transaction volume, and so on.

Photos App

All of the images you've taken with your iPhone will be displayed in the Photos app. You can also perform basic editing and erase obsolete or unattractive photos you no longer require.

Facetime

FaceTime is an Apple video and audio calling program that allows you to call your friends, family, acquaintances, and so on from anywhere on the globe for free. It uses network data and is only available on iOS-enabled mobile devices and Mac desktops.

Clips

The Clips app for the iPhone is an iOS app that allows you to make and share fascinating films with text, special effects, graphics, and so on.

TV App

A TV app also allows you to quickly find your favorite movies and TV series with a few finger presses. When you're on the go, the TV app gives you access to all accessible programming from your active streaming subscriptions and cable TV. It's like watching TV when you're not at home.

Music App

The music app is the last app on the dock of the iPhone. The iPhone Music app is a single-window software that lets you listen to all your downloaded music and songs from your music library. It also has a search bar for locating the best music and playlists.

Pages App

Pages is an iPhone's word-processing app that comes preloaded on the iPhone and allows you to create documents. You may collaborate with colleagues from around the globe using the Pages app.

Settings

The Settings app manages everything on your iPhone, from how it works to what information it exchanges with Apple-owned and third-party apps. It also governs your security and external device connection procedures.

For maximum functionality, different applications necessitate distinct configurations and settings. The Settings app allows you to customize these distinct sets of settings to serve each application's needs better.

Files

The Files app provides access to your files stored on online cloud services such as your iCloud account, Google Drive, Dropbox cloud storage, and any other cloud storage service, all in one place. You can browse the saved file directly on your iOS-enabled device and run various commands.

The Health App

The Health app lets you track your fitness progress over time. You can also create a medical ID, which will contain a record of your medical condition and could be invaluable in an emergency.

Home App

The Home app connects to and securely controls HomeKit-compatible smart home devices. You can categorize your accessories by room, control several accessories at once, use Siri to control your smart home appliances, and so on from within the app.

Weather app

The Weather app displays the current weather conditions in your location. It also shows forecasted weather conditions for the next few days. You may also use the weather app to find out what the weather is like in specific regions worldwide.

News App

The News app displays the most recent news stories from across the world. You can also use it to find location-specific news stories in any part of the world that pique your interest.

Phone App

On the bottom left of the iPhone dock is the *Phone* app. It is the app responsible for making and receiving voice calls. It has a *keypad* section that you can use to dial whatever number you are looking to call.

There is also a "*Favorites*" function in the *Phone* app (as shown below), which is a list of contacts you frequently call and have saved to your Favorites for easy access when you want to call any of them.

Your new iPhone has no contacts saved in "*Favorites*" fresh out of the box. However, if you've imported your *Contacts* data, along with other important data, from a previous iPhone that had some contacts saved as Favorites, those contacts will appear in the "Favorites" section of your new device as well. If you want to add a new contact from your contact list to your Favorites, just tap on the blue + sign at the top left corner of the Favorites screen.

The "*Recents*" section lists the recent calls you've made, while the "*voicemail*" section has any voicemails your callers left on those calls.

The *Contacts* icon, which is located in the middle of the icon row at the bottom of the *Phone* app screen, contains a complete list of your phone number contacts. You can tap on any contacts to give them a call, view your call history with them, or add them to your *Favorites*.

CHAPTER 4: SECURITY

Whether you've just bought an iPhone 14 or are upgrading your old iPhone operating system software, it's a good idea to stay up to date on Apple's latest changes, including how new features may benefit or harm your device's security and online privacy.

Malware can potentially compromise the security of your iPhone's devices and data. Malicious software includes naming a few viruses, worms, trojans, ransomware, and spyware. When you use the internet, receive email and text messages, or lose your iPhone, your security is at risk.

By knowing how to protect your iPhone operating system and getting familiar with any constraints, you can positively contribute to your iPhone and data security.

Are you in need of assistance? We will look at the many security options available and additional steps you can take to help keep your iPhone and its data safe and secure, and we will come up with some recommendations.

Separate Log-Ins for Each User Should Be Required

You probably don't want others to have administrative access to your iPhone if you aren't the only one who uses it. You can create multiple users on your iPhone, each of whom must log in separately. Other users will not be able to log in as administrators, but you will.

It prevents other users from accessing your files and settings while allowing you to protect yourself as an administrator. If your guests only use your computer occasionally, you can allow them to log in. You can also divide yourself up into groups.

Check That Your Privacy and Security Settings Are as Effective as They Can Be

Apple's security and privacy settings provide several options for improving your iPhone's security and privacy. These are some examples of such configurations:

- Using Location Services, you can control which apps have access to your location data and which do not.

- Contacts — By managing your contacts, you can control which apps can access your data.

- Photos — You can control which apps have access to your images.

Set up the Find My feature

If you have the Find My iPhone feature enabled, you may be able to locate it more easily if it is lost or stolen. This is how it's done. To begin, enable Location Services in your privacy settings and select Find My iPhone from the list of applications that can use your location.

Although this tool can help you locate your iPhone, it also allows you to remotely wipe the hard disk of your iPhone if it is lost or stolen.

Change the Privacy Settings in Safari to Your Preference

Furthermore, the Safari browser includes privacy settings that you can use to protect your internet activities from prying eyes. These are the privacy settings:

- Clear History from the Safari menu: This option clears the History menu's cookies and other cached data.

- Safari's Preferences > Privacy menu can help prevent websites from tracking your movements.

Make a Strong Password

Fraudsters will occasionally use your passwords to gain access to your personal information. It goes without saying that strong, one-of-a-kind passcodes are essential. The following recommendations, on the other hand, will assist you in keeping your passcodes private:

- No personally identifiable information should be collected or used.

- Avoid using your name, the names of your family members, or any other personally identifiable information in your message or post.

- Create your phrases.

Make Your Passwords as Long as Possible

To avoid identity theft, passwords should be changed regularly.

- A password should never be reused under any circumstances.

- Each account should have its password.

- It is not advisable to enter your passwords on a computer or network that is not your own.

To Keep Your Information Safe, Use a Password Manager

When creating complex passwords, a unique combination of uppercase and lowercase characters, digits, and symbols must be used; otherwise, the password will be insecure. The issue, in this case, is that each device and program requires creating a unique password. The temptation to reuse old passwords or create simple, similar passwords that are easy to remember is strong, but doing so makes hackers' guesses easier.

Examine User Reviews for Mobile Applications

When evaluating an app, it is a good idea to read app reviews before downloading it. Examining reviews can assist you in avoiding potentially dangerous applications and ensure that you install a reputable application onto your iPhone.

When Granting Permissions to Third-Party Applications, Exercise Caution

Proceed with caution when granting rights to an application. Check that the permissions you're granting are valid. Is it really necessary to have them in the app? What uses might it make of the information? Is there a compelling reason for an app, for example, to require access to your microphone, contacts, or social network profile?

Check Your Service Sharing Configuration to Ensure It Is Correct

It is a good idea to configure your sharing options to limit your sharing. The best way to protect yourself is to disable sharing for all services except those you require. Screen sharing, file sharing, printer sharing, Remote Login, Remote Management, Remote Apple Events (for iOS devices), Internet Sharing, Bluetooth Sharing, and Content Caching are just a few of the features.

The steps to enable and disable service sharing are as follows:

Go to System Preferences > Sharing and press Enter to access the Apple menu. You can enable or disable services using the toggle buttons on the left-hand pane. When you enable a service, you can choose whether to allow all users or only those you specify.

Be Cautious of Phishing Scams and Unexpected Pop-Up Windows

Malware can occasionally infiltrate your iPhone via email and text messaging. For example, in phishing scams, compromised emails or text messages that appear to be from a trusted source, such as your bank, but are fake messages from a fraudster are fairly common these days. When you open pop-up windows or click on other malicious websites that solicit personal information, phishers attempt to trick you into disclosing personal information about yourself.

Is there anything you can do to protect yourself from internet fraud schemes? It is never a good idea to open emails or attachments that appear suspicious or unsolicited. Never respond to them or click on them, and never provide personal information on a website you aren't sure is legitimate to begin with.

To establish whether a website is trustworthy and secure, it is best to practice always traveling directly to a secure "HTTPS" website rather than through a link provided by someone else.

CHAPTER 5: CAMERA SETTINGS

How to Use the Camera App

Mastering the camera app will help you capture stunning pictures and high-resolution photos that you can flaunt on the internet. This camera guide offers the important features to get you up and running with the Camera app in no time.

1. Access the Camera App via Control Center

2. Open the Control Center.

3. Click on the Camera tile to launch the app.

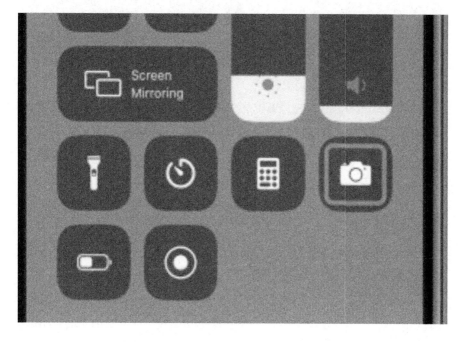

Switch Camera Modes

Once you launch the camera app, you can choose different camera modes. The camera mode for capturing images is different from that for shooting videos. For pictures, you have Pano, Photo, Portrait, etc., while for video, you have Slo-Mo, Time-Lapse, and Video.

Switching between the camera mode is easy. You can access the various camera modes in the horizontal scrolling menu at the app's bottom.

By default, it is set to Photo mode. You must swipe right to change to Video or another video mode, such as Slo-Mo.

Swipe left to revert to Photo or to select another photo mode.

Switch to the Front-Facing Camera

The front-facing camera lets you capture selfies without guessing too much, unlike the rear-facing camera. Switching from the rear-facing to the front-facing camera is easy. Regardless of the camera, you can also swipe left or right on the horizontal scrolling menu to choose your preferred camera mode.

To switch to the front camera, click on the front-facing camera button (i.e., the camera icon with two split arrows heading in the same direction) in the lower right of the app.

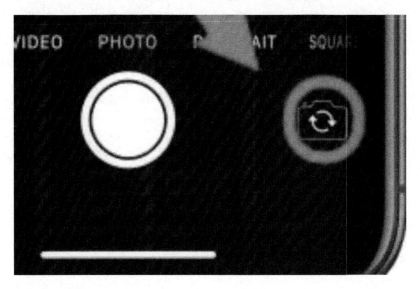

Adjust Exposure

If you observe, you will see a yellow square lurking over your subject. Click on your subject on the display if you don't see it.

There is a sun icon next to the yellow square; you can use this to change the image's exposure, i.e., make the photo brighter or darker.

Click on the yellow sun icon to bring out the vertical slider.

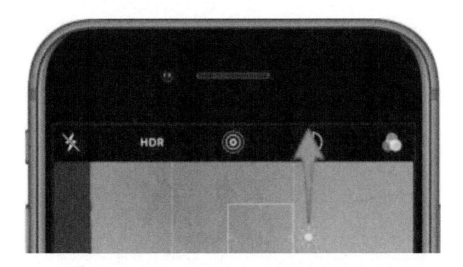

Increase the exposure by sliding up (brighter) or decrease it by sliding down (darker).

Remove your fingers from there if you're okay with the lighting.

After choosing your subject and adjusting the exposure, you can decide to lock onto your subject so that even if you mistakenly toss your phone, your subject and exposure will remain the same. Hold down in the middle of the yellow square icon until the AE/AF Lock button appears on the display's top.

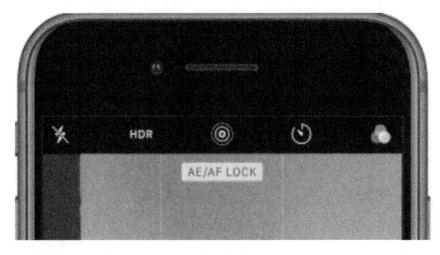

- AE = Auto Exposure

- AF = Auto Focus

Even after you've captured a photo, the AE/AF Lock will remain intact, allowing you to keep capturing photos at your desired settings.

Click anywhere within your field of view to undo the AE/AF Lock.

How to Use the Auto and Manual Flash

If you've taken a picture in a camera app before, you will observe that the camera sometimes uses the phone's flashlight to make the captured image look brighter. It also applies to the camera app on the iPhone. Auto Flash allows the camera to choose when to capture with a flashlight or do it manually.

1. If you need to adjust the Flash settings, click on the Flash (lightning bolt) button at the upper left.

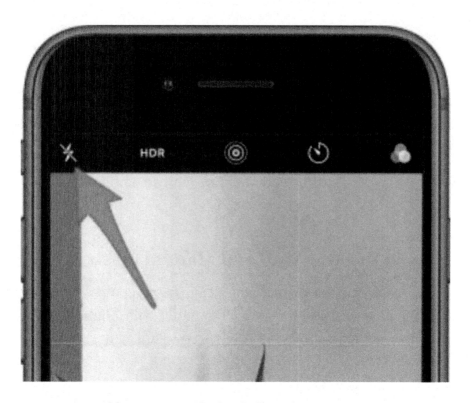

2. To enable automatic flash, click *Auto*.

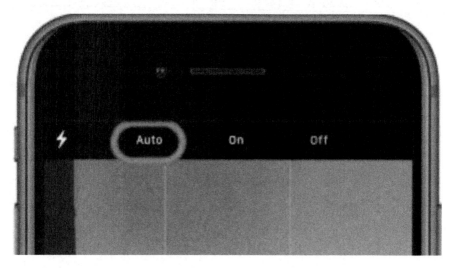

3. To enable your flash, click *On*.

4. To disable flash, click *Off*.

How to Use the Shutter Button

Once you are set to take a picture or video, you can do it by using your phone's volume key or the shutter button in the Camera app.

If you need to take a picture or record a video using the volume controls, start framing your shot/video and tap the volume up/volume down key to take the picture or record the video.

If you need to take a photo with the shutter button, begin framing your image and tapping the large white circle at the bottom of the app.

Suppose you need to record a video, first frame it, and then click the red icon at the bottom of the part. Following that, the circle will turn white. To stop the recording, click it again.

You can also take a Burst photo by pressing the shutter button. If you're wondering what the heck Burst photos are, read on. They are a series of photographs taken in rapid succession.

1. Long-press the shutter button to capture a burst image.

2. Hold the shutter button for a few seconds, then release your fingers.

3. Launch the Photos app to find your burst photo collection.

4. Choose the pictures you need to keep and delete the rest.

View the Captured Photo

To see the pictures you have taken using the camera app, you will need to exit the app and go over to the Photos app. But wait, here's a tip: you can access the Photos app directly from the

Camera app. Click the small thumbnail at the lower left of the camera app to see your recently captured pictures and videos.

Take Live Photos

A Live Photo functions similarly to a GIF. It lets your camera shoot a few seconds of video and sound to produce a short clip of moving images. You can find the Live Photo button at the top of the camera screen.

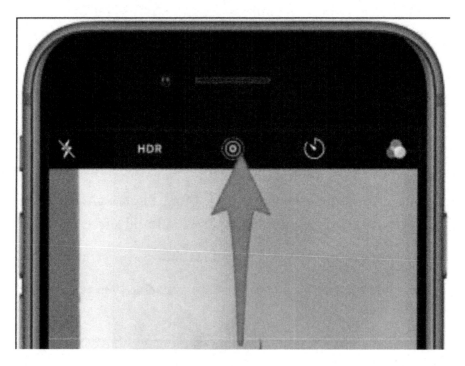

Edit your Pictures in Batch

The batch editing feature first appears in iOS 16. It allows users to customize a single image and then quickly apply those changes to an entire album's worth of photos. It means that changes made to one image can be easily copied and pasted into another or several images at once. It also implies that changes like brightness, shadows, and exposure will be copied and pasted onto the new photos.

How to Get Rid of Duplicate Photos

Unless you regularly filter the photos in your Photos app, they will likely contain duplicates. While it's not the end of the world, having a lot of duplicates can be inconvenient when trying to sort through memories or find a specific picture.

Before iOS 16, removing duplicate photos from the Photos app was difficult. Duplicates in the Photos app are now easier to remove in iOS 16. If you don't want to delete duplicate photos, you can merge them. It ensures that no photos are lost while reducing the size of your photo library.

Record a Video

1. Navigate to Camera and swipe to select "*Video mode*."

2. Then, click the Record button. Otherwise, tap any of the volume keys to begin recording. There are a few things you can do while videoing.

3. Now, click the white Shutter icon to capture a still image.

4. Pinch the display to zoom in/out.

5. For further accurate zooming, long-press *1x*, and then push the slider towards the left.

6. Click the Record icon; otherwise, click any volume keys to end videoing.

You can adjust the frame rates and video resolution: Navigate to Settings and click on "*Camera*," then click "*Record Video*."

Record in Cinematic Mode

Cinematic mode lets you blur the background while keeping the subject sharp during a video.

1. Navigate to the camera and choose Cinematic mode.

2. Optional: Click **1x** before the shooting to zoom in.

3. To change the depth-of-field, click on the ___ Depth Adjustment icon and then push the slider towards the left/ right before shooting.

4. To begin recording, click the Record icon or press any volume controls.

5. A yellow frame on the interface indicates that the subject is in focus, whereas a gray frame indicates that the subject is recognized but not in focus. Click the gray button to adjust the focus; click again to keep the focus on the subject steady.

6. If no one appears in the video, click somewhere on the screen to make it the main focus.

7. Long-press the display to lock the focus at a particular distance.

8. Click the Record icon to end the shoot.

Record a Slow-Motion Video

A video in slow-mo mode will record as usual, but you can only see the slow-motion effect anytime you play it back.

1. Navigate to the camera and swipe to Slo-mo mode. Or, click

the Camera Back-Facing icon to shoot Slo-mo videos using the front camera.

2. Click on the Record icon to begin videoing.

3. If needed, click the Shutter icon to capture a still image while videoing.

4. Click the Record icon again to end the recording.

If you want a section of the video to play in slow motion while leaving the rest at normal speed, click on the video thumbnail, and choose "*Edit.*" Drag the vertical bars under the viewer to map the portion you wish to play back in slow-motion.

To adjust the slo-mo mode frame rate and resolution: Navigate to Settings and choose "*Camera.*" Then click on "*Record Slo-mo.*"

Change the Camera's Focus and Exposure

The iPhone's camera automatically locks the focus and exposure, but if you need to do it manually, here's what to do:

1. Navigate to Camera.

2. Click on display to show the automatic focus section and exposure setting.

3. Now, click on where you wish to pin the focus area.

4. Slide the Adjust Exposure icon next to the focus section up or down to change the exposure.

5. To steady the manual focus and exposure settings for future recordings, long-press the focus section until the *AE/AF Lock* button shows up; click the display to unlock settings.

6. You can accurately configure and stabilize the exposure for future recordings. Click the Camera Controls icon and

the Exposure button. Now, drag the slider to change the exposure. The exposure will remain that way for subsequent shots. You can still save it, so it doesn't reset when you launch the Camera app. Navigate to Settings, click the Camera option, and then choose "*Preserve Settings*." Now, toggle on "*Exposure Adjustment*."

Enable/Disable the Camera's Flash

The camera app will automatically turn on the flash when you take a picture that needs more illumination. You can manually set the flash before taking a photo. Here's how:

1. Click on the Flash button to activate or deactivate the

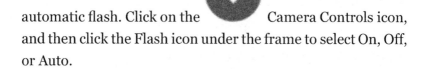

automatic flash. Click on the ⌄ Camera Controls icon, and then click the Flash icon under the frame to select On, Off, or Auto.

Capture a Photo with a Filter

Filters are tools used to add color effects to photos, and you can use them on the camera app to give your photo a stunning look.

1. Navigate to Camera.

2. Swipe to Photo or Portrait mode.

3. Now, click on the ⌄ Camera Controls icon.

4. Click the Filters icon.

5. Swipe left or right under the viewer to see a preview of the filters, and click one to use it.

Use the Timer

The camera app has a timer button that you can tap to give you more time before the shot is taken.

1. To configure the timer, navigate to Camera.

2. Click on the ⌄ Camera Controls icon and Timer icon.

3. Now, select *3s* or *10s*.

4. Afterward, hit the Shutter icon to start the timer.

Use Grid to Straighten Your Photos

Adding a grid to the camera interface can help you to straighten and adjust your shot.

1. Select the Settings application.

2. Select "Camera."

3. Now, select "Grid."

4. After you've taken a photo, use the editing tools in the Photos app to fine-tune it and change the horizontal and vertical orientation.

Take Macro Photographs and Videos

The ultra-wide camera can take macro photos and videos.

1. Navigate to the camera and go 2cm closer to the subject to allow the camera to lock in focus automatically.

Enable/Disable HDR Video

2. Navigate to Settings.

3. Click on "*Camera*."

4. Now, click "*Record Video*."

5. Toggle on or off "*HDR Video*."

6. Take Burst Mode Shots

7. Burst mode lets you take a shot of a moving subject or multiple

high-speed pictures at once, so you can have different images to pick from.

CHAPTER 6: BASIC IPHONE CONTROLS

Using Hardware Buttons

The hardware button is the conventional way of shutting down the iPhone without tapping the screen. It is helpful if your phone's screen is damaged or not responding and you need to switch it off.

1. To shut down, long-press the Side button and the Volume Up button until the power off slider appears on the screen.

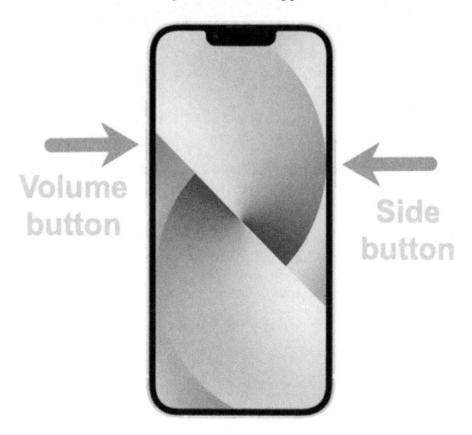

2. Then, push the "*slide to power off*" tile towards the right side.

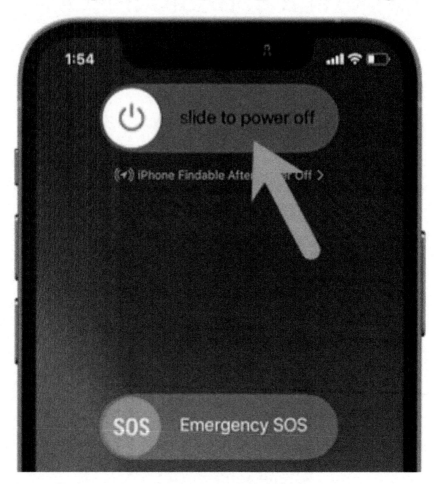

3. Once done, your phone will shut down.

4. Hold down the Side button for some seconds to power it on until the Apple logo comes up on the screen.

Without Power Button

Few people know you can shut down the iPhone from the Settings app. Well, you're one of the lucky ones to know this trick.

1. Navigate the Settings app.

2. Then, click "*General.*"

3. Scroll down and press "*Shut Down.*"

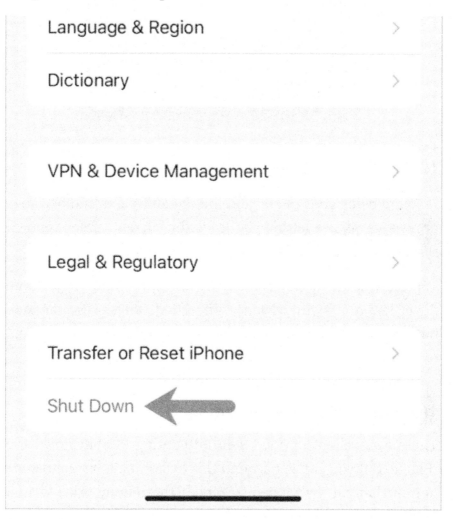

4. Push the slider to turn off the iPhone.

How to Force Restart your iPhone

If you're using your phone and the screen freezes and becomes unresponsive, not letting you leave the current screen, a force restart can help troubleshoot such a problem.

Tap the volume up key and swiftly let go, then tap the volume down key and swiftly let go. After that, long-press the side button till Apple's logo comes up. Then, hold on for the phone to restart.

How to Restart your iPhone

There's no reboot option when attempting to shut down the iPhone, but you can get around this by adding a virtual restart button that can be tapped to reboot the iPhone. This virtual button is called AssistiveTouch.

1. Navigate to the Settings app.

2. Now, click "**_Accessibility_**."

3. From here, click "**_Touch_**."

4. At this point, click on "**_AssistiveTouch_**" and toggle on its switch to enable it.

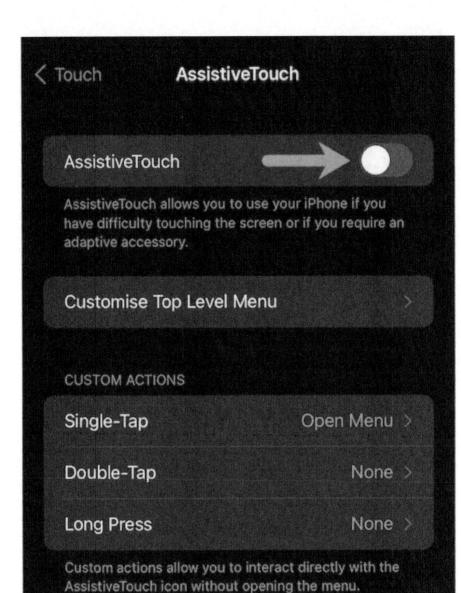

5. Once done, the AssistiveTouch digital button will show up on the display.

6. Click on the button and press "**Device**."

7. Now, tap the triple dots.

8. Click on "**Restart**" and then choose restart to confirm.

9. Once done, your phone will automatically restart.

Restore the Backup

After erasing your iPhone's content, you can get them back from the backup when you try to set up your iPhone again. Here's how to do it.

1. To turn on the phone, press the side key. Once turned on, you should see the "Hello" screen, just as you did when setting up your iPhone.

2. Follow the onscreen prompts until you reach the Apps & Data page.

3. Then, select "Restore from iCloud Backup."

4. To proceed, enter the Apple ID and password associated with your iCloud account.

5. When the "Terms and Conditions" interface appears, select "Agree."

6. Make a choice from your backups based on your preferences.

7. Allow a few minutes for the recovery process to complete.

8. Once complete, you can now see your previously backed-up data, such as pictures, apps, documents, etc., on your new iPhone.

Adding the Quick Note Icon to Control Center

First, you'll have to add the Quick Note shortcut to the Control Center to be easier to access. Here's how:

1. Select the Settings application.

2. Click "Control Center" now.

3. Below the "More Controls" submenu, click the green "+" icon next to "Quick Note." Following that, the Quick Note icon will appear in the Control Center.

How to Make a Quick Note

Making a Quick Note is as simple as tapping the shortcut after adding the Quick Note symbol to your phone's Control Center. The steps are as follows:

1. Go to the Control Center.

2. Now, click on the Quick Note shortcut.

3. Afterward, the Quick Note interface will show up on your iPhone screen to allow you to write down your ideas or whatever you feel like taking note of.

4. After making a note, click on "*Save*" in the right-most corner.

Saving a Safari Website Link to Quick Note

If you see a compelling article while surfing the web, you can copy and paste the URL into a Quick Note on your device.

Navigate to Voice Memos.

1. Now, click on the triple-dot button beside your recording.

2. Then, choose "*New Quick Note.*"

3. Pen down your thoughts and click "*Save*" after doing so.

Access and View All Your Quick Notes

You may be curious about where you can find your saved Quick Notes on your phone. Well, you shouldn't bother. The Notes app on iOS 16 has a Quick Notes folder that contains all your saved Quick Notes.

Enable Dark Mode with a Focus

Focus Filters also let you apply system-wide changes to your iPhone screen. For instance, if you add Dark Mode to your Sleep Focus mode, it will activate dark mode on your phone when the sleep mode is initiated. Your phone's screen will become dark and more appealing to the eyes.

1. Launch the Settings app.

2. Click on *Focus*.

3. Then, click on the Focus mode (we choose Wind Down) for which you want Dark Mode to be turned on.

☾   Do Not Disturb   ›

🛏   Sleep   ›

🎓   Studying   ›

🌅   Wind Down   ›

📵   Work   ›

👤   Personal   Set Up ›

Focus lets you customise your devices and silence calls and notifications. Turn it on and off in Control Centre.

Share Across Devices

Focus is shared across your devices, and turning one on for this device will turn it on for all of them.

4.   Locate the "*Focus Filters*" section, and click *Add Filter*.

5. After that, click the Dark Mode tile below the "**System Filters**" heading.

6. Ensure that Dark is displayed on the "**Appearance**" selection, and click *Add*.

7. With these settings, Dark Mode will automatically be applied to your phone whenever you turn on Focus mode.

Enable Focus Mode

If you've had enough of being interrupted by alerts when trying to focus on a task, or even worse, while trying to fall asleep, then the Focus Mode can help. You can set the time, the people, and the types of notifications you see when using the focus modes.

1. Open the Control Center.

2. Click on the Focus tile in the left column close to the middle. It will show your most recent Focus mode if any.

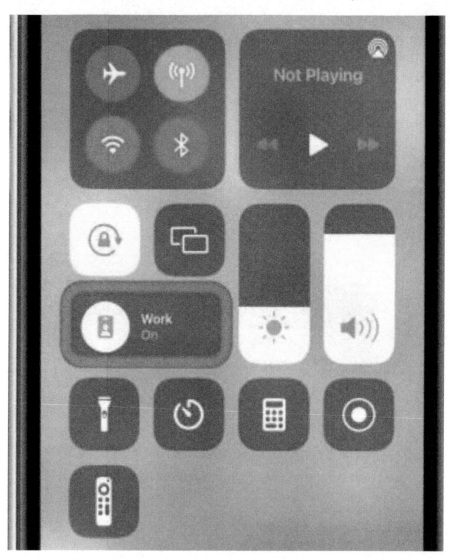

3. After that, click on Work, Sleep, Do Not Disturb, or any other Focus mode.

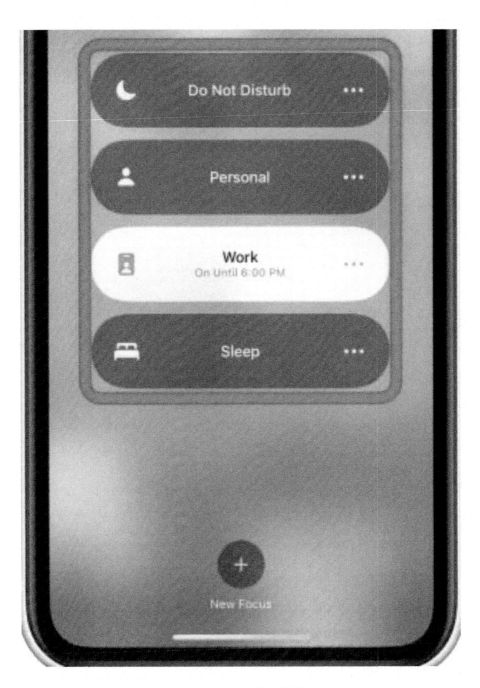

4. To create a custom Focus mode, click on **New Focus**.

Adjust The Volume on iPhone

You can adjust the audio level on your iPhone while on the phone or while listening to songs, movies, or other media. The level for the ringer, alerts and other sound effects is controlled via the buttons while not in use. Siri can also be used to increase or decrease the volume.

You can say, "Turn the volume up" or "Turn the volume down," to Siri, for example.

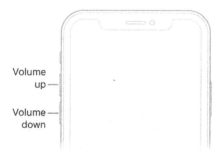

In Settings, you may lock the ringer and alert volume.

1. Go to the Settings menu.

2. Choose between Sounds and Haptics (on supported models) and Sounds (on other iPhone models).

3. Turn off the Change with Buttons option.

4. Adjust the volume in Control Center.

5. When your iPhone is locked or using an app, you can control the volume in Control Center.

6. Open The Control Center, then drag.

Silence Calls, Alarms, and Notifications for the Time Being.

Toggle between Focus and Do Not Disturb in Control Center. (See the Do Not Disturb setting.)

Set your iPhone to silent mode.

Set the Ring/Silent switch to orange to put the iPhone in silent mode. Set the switch back to turn off silent mode.

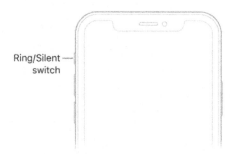

Ring/Silent switch

All sounds are played when the iPhone's silent mode is turned off. iPhone does not ring or play notifications or other sound effects when in silent mode (but iPhone may still vibrate).

Important: Even when silent mode is on, clock alarms, audio programs like Music, and many games play sounds through the built-in speaker. Even when the Ring/Mute switch is set to silent in some countries or areas, the sound effects for the Camera, Voice Memos, and Emergency Alerts are played.

Change Name on Your iPhone

Why would you want to rename your iPhone?

While the name of your iPhone may appear to be hidden, it can be revealed in a few circumstances. When you connect your iPhone to a Bluetooth device, such as a car stereo, your phone's name may appear on the screen. When your phone is connected to a computer, your name may appear in iCloud backups, Airdrop, and when connected to a computer.

Perhaps you gave your iPhone a bad name and now want to change it. Perhaps you simply want to spice up your life.

Whatever your reason, here's how to change the name of your iPhone.

1. The first step in renaming your iPhone is to open the Settings app. This app is most likely on your home screen, but if you can't find it, use the search function on your phone by swiping it down from the top of your screen. Then, type "settings" in the search field to find the settings app.

2. After you've opened the Settings app on your iPhone, navigate to the "General" tab. Here you will find a variety of phone settings.

3. After you've navigated to the General menu, click "About." The About page contains a wealth of information about your phone, including the serial number.

4. When you get to the About page:

5. On this page, select Name from the drop-down menu.

6. Change the name of your iPhone and then select "done" to save the new name.

That's all there is to it! Changing the name of your iPhone is straightforward, whether you want it to be more covert or more particular.

Change Time on Your iPhone

Time for auto-update (NITZ)

Your device's default configuration changes the time zone automatically. Follow these steps to set the device clock to automatically update, depending on the time zone it is in:

1. Tap Settings > General > Date and Time from the Home screen.

2. Toggle the Set Automatically slider on or off.

3. Decide on a time and date.

4. Tap Settings > General > Date and Time from the Home screen.

5. Toggle the Set Automatically slider to the off position.

6. Select your time zone by tapping the current time zone.

7. To select the correct day and time, tap the date or time and scroll up or down.

Change the Language on Your iPhone

If the language setting on your iPad, iPhone, or iPod touch is incorrect, or you've mistakenly changed it to a language you don't understand, you can change it.

1. Tap Settings on the Home screen.

2. Tap General on the following screen.

3. Tap "[Device] Language" on the following screen.

4. Choose your preferred language.

5. You'll receive an alert asking you to confirm the new language. The first choice should be selected.

6. After your device updates the language, your device should automatically display the one you selected.

How to Customize Control Center

Control Center is most useful when it contains only the shortcuts you use. You can edit the bottom row of icons, including removing or adding shortcuts and rearranging their arrangement.

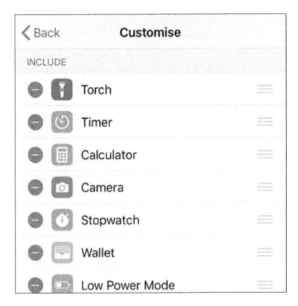

1. To modify Control Center, follow these steps:

2. Go to Settings > Control Center on your iPhone.

3. Tap "Customize Controls" to see a list of available shortcuts.

4. Drag items from the "More Controls" column to the "Include" button to activate them. Do the inverse to deactivate a shortcut.

5. You can also rearrange objects by moving them around. Each line in Control Center can have up to four shortcuts.

6. While configuring, you can use the relevant gesture to display the Control Center and check how things look.

7. Long-Pressing in the Control Center gives you more options.

Control Center has more to it than meets the eye. You can access hidden submenus with a long press (tap and hold) on practically any shortcut.

To see even more possibilities, press and hold the wireless controllers for a long time. You can control other devices by long-pressing the "Now Playing" box. Many custom shortcuts include hidden options that can be accessed by long-pressing them.

Make a Screen Recording

You had to connect your iPhone to a Mac and record with QuickTime until Apple introduced a true screen recording feature. Thankfully, recording on your device is now a lot easier.

To do so, follow the steps outlined above to enable the Screen Recording shortcut. Simply press "Screen Recording" to begin recording when you've done so.

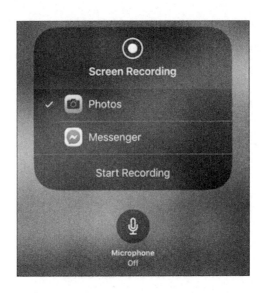

If you long-press the "Screen Recording" shortcut, you may be able to select Photos (the default) or another app. You can share your screen with apps that support it.

You can also activate the microphone (which is disabled by default). Tap the red area at the top of the screen to stop a continuous screen recording or broadcast.

Lock the screen in portrait mode.

One of the Control Center's most useful shortcuts is to the left of the Do-Not-Disturb moon. This setting may lock your screen in Portrait mode when you move your smartphone sideways, preventing it from transitioning to Landscape mode — or vice versa.

It is especially beneficial when you're lying down and using your phone. Because some folks do not like Landscape mode, they always prefer their device to be in Portrait mode.

Toggle Night Shift, Dark Mode, or True Tone

In Control Center, you can long-press almost everything. Long-pressing the Brightness slider has several useful settings for switching between Light and Dark themes, enabling "Night Shift" and disabling "True Tone."

If you're unfamiliar with these options, "Night Shift" helps you fall asleep by limiting your exposure to blue light. "True Tone" automatically adjusts your display's white balance to reflect the ambient white balance in your surroundings.

Manually adjust screen brightness

1. Move the "Brightness" button in the Control Center.

2. Move the slider to "Settings" > "Screen and Brightness."

3. Screen brightness can be adjusted automatically.

4. Navigate to "Settings" > "Accessibility."

5. Turn on "Automatically adjust brightness" under "Screen and text size."

How to Create a Passcode

Passwords on the iPhone are referred to as Passcode. If you

need to protect your device from others, here's how to enable a passcode.

1. Go to the Settings menu.

2. Click "Face ID & Passcode" now.

3. Click "Turn On Passcode" from here.

4. Enter your 6-digit passcode or select "Passcode Options" for other options.

5. To confirm, enter the same passcode again.

6. Toggle any option under the "ALLOW ACCESS WHEN LOCKED" heading on or off.

Change Your Password

Here's how to remove your current passcode and replace it with a new one.

1. Go to the Settings menu.

2. Click "Face ID & Passcode" now.

3. If prompted, enter your current passcode.

4. Scroll to the bottom and click "Change Passcode."

5. After that, enter the current passcode.

6. Select "Passcode Options."

7. Make your choice, enter your new passcode, and then re-enter it.

8. Then press the "Done" button.

Disable the Passcode

1. Go to the Settings menu.

2. Click "Face ID & Passcode" now.

3. Select "Turn Passcode Off."

Volume

Adjust the volume on your iPhone using this option.

How to Enable AirDrop

You must enable AirDrop on the devices between which you want to transfer files for it to work. You only need to do this once per device, after which you can transfer files between them at any time.

When Using a Mac

1. Tap the Finder icon in the Dock at the bottom of the screen.

2. Tap on AirDrop at the left of the sidebar.

3. If your Mac's Bluetooth or Wi-Fi is turned off, you will be prompted to turn it on.

4. Select who can bring you AirDrop in the AirDrop window. Select Contacts Only or All under "Allow me to be discovered by."

If Finder is open, you can also tap Go in the menu bar at the top of your screen, followed by the AirDrop drop-down menu.

On the iPhone and iPad

1. Launch the Settings app on your phone.

2. Select General.

3. Select AirDrop.

4. Choose whether you want "Contacts Only" or "Everyone" to be discoverable.

Limiting AirDrop to your contacts is safer, but selecting "everyone" is easier if you receive files from various people. If you select "everyone," keep in mind that if you work in a public place, anyone nearby can send you files, so be cautious about who you receive your AirDrop files.

Making Phone Calls

There are two ways to make a call from the Phone application. You can manually enter the phone number or call someone from your contacts or favorites list.

To dial a number:

1. Open the phone app by clicking its icon in the Dock at the bottom of the home screen.

2. Click on the keypad tab at the bottom of the screen and enter the phone number you want to call.

3. Click on the green Call to make a call.

4. When the call is over, tap the red End button to close it.

In some applications, such as Email and Safari, you can call a phone number by simply tapping the number or call button.

To call a contact:

1. Instead of manually dialing the number, you can save the phone number to your phone as a contact. The lessons on adding and managing contacts will go into more detail about contacts.

2. Open the phone app. The list of contacts you've saved will be displayed.

3. Click the Contacts ![icon] tab at the base of the screen, and then click on the name of the contact you wish to call. If you have a lot of contacts, you can use the row of Alphabets on the right to move to contacts that begin with a particular letter quickly.

4. Click on the desired contact's phone number to make your call.

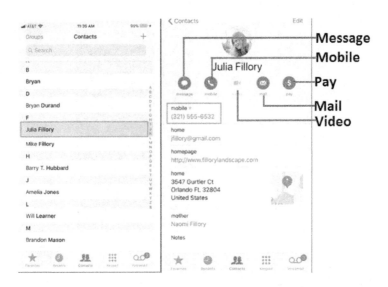

5. The next screen will contain details of this contact. You can add other details on this screen by tapping Edit at the top right of the screen.

6. To call your friend, click on mobile.

7. When the call ends, tap End to end it.

Answering and Rejecting Calls

If your phone is in lock screen mode and you receive a call, you can choose to answer or reject it. Drag the green phone to answer the incoming call. To turn off the ringtone, press the side button. Press the side button twice to reject the call and send it directly to voice mail.

If you're already using your iPhone, click *Accept* to answer the call or click *Decline* to reject the call.

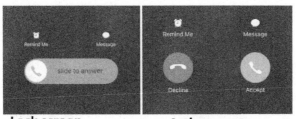

Lock screen   **Active screen**

You can also tap *Message* to reply with a text message or *Remind Me* to schedule a reminder to call that contact later.

CHAPTER 7: APPLE PAY

Set Up Apple Pay

Using Apple Pay may be more convenient and secure than a traditional credit card. If your cards are saved in the Wallet app, you can use Apple Pay to make secure payments in stores, public transportation, apps, and websites that accept Apple Pay. Send and receive money from friends and family using Apple Pay in Messages, and make purchases at participating merchants.

Add your debit, credit, and prepaid cards to Wallet to set up Apple Pay.

Add a Credit or Debit Card

Tap the Add Card button in Wallet. You may be required to provide your Apple ID credentials.

Choose one of the following options:

1. Select the card associated with your Apple ID, cards used with Apple Pay on other devices, or cards previously deleted. Continue, then enter the CVV number for each card.

2. Place your iPhone, so your debit or credit card is visible in the frame, or manually enter the card information.

3. You may also be able to add your card using your bank's or card issuer's app.

4. The card issuer determines whether your card is Apple Pay compatible and may require additional information from you to complete the verification process.

Rearrange Your Cards and Set the Default Card

The default payment method is the first card added to Wallet. To make another card the default, move it to the top of the stack.

1. In Wallet, set your default card.

2. Before dragging the card to the top of the stack, touch and hold it.

3. To rearrange a card, touch and hold it, then drag it to a new location.

4. Apple Pay and its functionalities are not available in every nation or area.

Configure and Use Apple Cash on Your iPhone

With Apple Cash, you can use Apple Pay to make purchases, send and receive money via the Wallet and Messages apps, and transfer your Apple Cash balance to your bank account.

Set Up Apple Cash

Perform any of the subsequent:

1. To enable Apple Cash, go to Settings > Wallet & Apple Pay > Apple Cash.

2. Launch the Wallet application, press the Apple Cash card, and then hit Setup Now.

You may give or receive money through Messages.

Send Money with Apple Cash

1. Tap Send after selecting the Apple Cash card in Wallet.

2. Enter an addressee or select a recent contact, then click Next.

3. Enter the desired amount, then click the Send with Messages button.

4. Add a remark if desired, then click the Send button.

5. Examine the payment information before authenticating with Face ID, Touch ID, or PIN.

6. Additionally, you may submit payment using Messages.

Request Money with Apple Cash

1. Hit the Apple Cash card in Wallet, then tap Request.

2. Enter an addressee or select a recent contact, then click Next.

3. Enter the desired amount, then click Request with Messages.

4. Add a remark if desired, then click the Send button.

5. The funds you receive are applied to your Apple Cash balance.

6. You can also request payment via Messages.

Transfer Money from Your Debit Card to Your Wallet

Deposit money into your bank account. To learn how to transfer Apple Cash funds to a bank account or debit card, visit the Apple Support page.

Choose whether payments should be taken manually or automatically. If you accept payments manually, you have seven days before the money is returned to the sender.

Update your banking account information.

For help, contact Apple Support.

Look at your proposed PIN number. Apple Cash does not require a PIN because every transaction is authenticated using Face ID, Touch ID, or a secure password. However, some terminals may still require a four-digit code to complete the transaction.

Make a Statement Request

Identify yourself to maintain your account and increase your transaction limits.

View Statements and Transactions

In Wallet, tap Apple Card.

Carry out any of the following:

- Examine your transactions: Get a list of your most recent transactions, or scroll down for a list of all your transactions organized by month and year.

- To search your transactions, click the Search button, type your query, and tap the Search key. You can also select a recommended search, such as a category, merchant, or area, and then enter additional text to narrow your search.

·   Check out the weekly, monthly, or annual activity: Tap Activity (below Card Balance) to see a breakdown of your spending by categories, such as Shopping, Food & Beverage, and Services. For a fresh perspective, select Week, Month, or Year. Swipe right to see previous periods.

·   Tap Card Balance to see the balance, new purchases, payments, and credits and to receive monthly statements.

·   To view your monthly statements, scroll down. Tap a statement to see the month's summary, download a PDF statement, or export transactions to a CSV, OFX, QFX, or QBO file.

Access Wallet & Apple Pay on the Lock screen

You no longer need to unlock your iPhone to make contactless payments. All you have to do is double-tap the side key to open the Wallet app. You'll have to enable it beforehand. Here's how:

1. Launch the Settings app.

2. After that, click *Wallet & Apple Pay*.

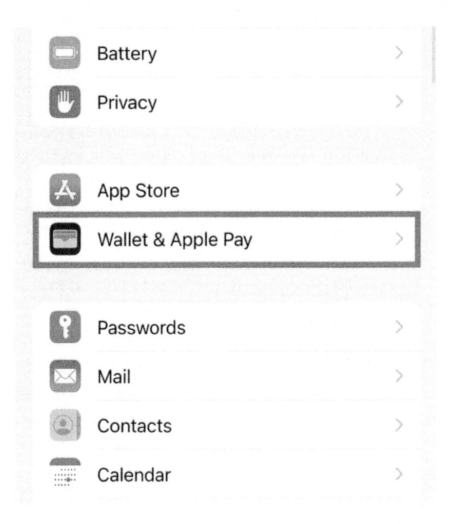

	Battery	>
	Privacy	>
	App Store	>
	Wallet & Apple Pay	>
	Passwords	>
	Mail	>
	Contacts	>
	Calendar	>

3. From there, click the "***Double-Click Side Button***" toggle to turn ON or OFF the feature. It's already ON by default.

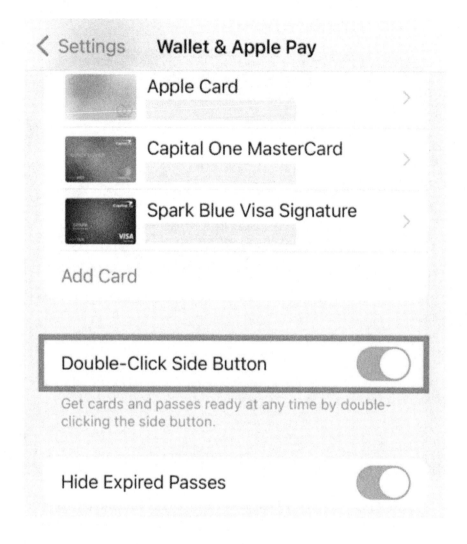

Apple Card   ›

Capital One MasterCard   ›

Spark Blue Visa Signature   ›

Add Card

Double-Click Side Button

Get cards and passes ready at any time by double-clicking the side button.

Hide Expired Passes

Add your ID to Apple Wallet

You can add your driver's license or state's identification to the Wallet app on your iPhone if your state approves Wallet IDs. You must note that Apple Wallet needs confirmation from your state's vehicle management. So, before you try to get through the checkpoint at an airport, ensure you allow adequate time to be given the go-ahead.

1. Launch the Wallet app.

2. Click on the plus (+) icon.

3. Find the "***Driver's License or State ID***" title and choose your state. If your state doesn't appear on the list, it means that it's not part of the program. However, if you see your state, click on it.

4. After that, select if you want to add your ID to your iPhone only or both the iPhone and Apple Watch.

5. Follow the prompt and scan the front of your ID.

6. Proceed also to scan the back of the ID.

7. Next, click "***Continue.***"

8. When you see the *"Additional Verification"* page, click *"Continue"* once more.

9. Follow the prompts to capture a photo of yourself.

10. After that, click *"Continue with Face ID."* Your selfie and ID credentials will be forwarded to your state's issuing management.

11. Click *"Done."*

Once you've been verified, you will get a notification on the Wallet app informing you that your digital ID is okay to use for certain airport checkpoints.

CHAPTER 8:
TROUBLESHOOTING, TIPS, AND TRICKS

Troubleshooting Common Problems

Activation issues

Activation issues are basic when you attempt to get another telephone fully operational just because, paying little mind to show, and the iPhone 14 has demonstrated to be the same

Potential arrangements:

If you're having trouble activating your new iPhone 14, check Apple's System Status page to ensure that all frameworks are ready for action. If something is not turned on the green, wait until all frameworks are up, and then try again. If it's still green and unusable, check to see if your phone has a SIM card embedded. On the off chance that you can switch the SIM card from your old telephone to your new one, try that first. Apple recommends the following steps if you receive a "No SIM" or "Invalid SIM" error message.

1. Ensure your remote arrangement is operational.

2. Restart your device after updating to the most recent iOS version.

3. Navigate to Setting > General > About. If an update is available, you'll see a prompt to choose OK or Update and then update.

4. Remove your SIM card from the plate and replace it. The plate should securely close. Use the plate that came with your current phone, as others may not fit.

5. Attempt an alternate SIM card. You can get one at your transporter's retail outlet or request that your bearer test your telephone with an alternate card. Supplant your current SIM card with another one if necessary.

Volume, Sound, and Sound Issues

If you discover there are issues with any part of sound capacity, there are different cures you can attempt.

Potential arrangements:

· Remove your SIM card from your telephone, and afterward change it to fix the issue of an inadequately situated card.

· Mood killer Bluetooth to contrast sound quality or without it. On the off chance that it improves, leave it off for your calls.

· Ensure your receiver is perfect, clear, and unhindered.

· If the above advances don't improve the sound, clear your telephone's reserved memory by restarting it.

· Do a hard manufacturing plant reset (Settings > General > Reset). Before proceeding to this, make sure to back up your information first.

Bluetooth association issues

Various iPhone 14 users have reported problems connecting their Bluetooth peripherals. The issues include associating, interacting in the vehicle, and maintaining an association after initially interacting. The new iPhone 14 on iOS 16 is experiencing Bluetooth network issues. Associating isn't the problem. The problem is keeping the association together. In addition, I'm experiencing network issues in my vehicle. It will associate for 5 minutes or more before naturally disengaging and reconnecting. It's truly vexing.

Possible arrangements:

- Apple suggests several steps you can take before contacting technical support. Make a point to update your iOS to the most recently released version.

- Go to Settings > Bluetooth on your device and make sure Bluetooth is turned on. If it is disabled and unable to enable it, restart your iOS device. At that point, try combining and interacting again.

- Ascertain that your Bluetooth frill and device are nearby.

- Turn your Bluetooth frill on and off as needed.

- Check that your Bluetooth accessory is turned on, fully charged, or connected to power. If your extra battery needs to be replaced, try replacing it with new batteries. If you had the option to associate previously, unpair the frill and put it back in revelation mode before attempting to match and interface again.

If you can combine your adornment with different gadgets yet not your iOS gadget, unpair the embellishment from different gadgets and attempt again.

iPhone Won't Turn ON

Whenever you try to turn ON your iPhone, and it doesn't power On, it is either a software or hardware problem.

When you encounter this problem, you should first troubleshoot the software on your device. If the software has crashed, your iPhone may not turn on.

Force-resetting your iPhone 14 is the quickest way to troubleshoot your software. It is accomplished by pressing and quickly releasing the Volume Up button. Then, press and immediately release the Volume Down button, followed by the Power button, until the device restarts.

Another method is to simultaneously press and hold the Power and Home buttons until the iPhone 14 turns off and reboots. This action completely shuts down the iPhone.

A non-invasive software fix is ideal because it does not affect your personal information and resets everything in your Settings App. To accomplish this, follow these steps: To begin, select Erase All Content and Settings. Next, enter your Passcode and confirm by tapping Erase iPhone. Once the reset is complete, your iPhone will restart. It resolves any issues you may be experiencing with your software.

If you still keep encountering the same problem after following the steps above, what you should do as a matter of last resort is to carry out a DFU Restore. The DFU can be carried out following the steps outlined below:

1. First, connect your iPhone 14 to a PC with iTunes installed.

2. Next, press and hold the *Power and Home* button simultaneously for about 10 seconds.

3. After 10 seconds, still keep holding the *Home button* while you release the Power button.

4. You should see detailed information on iTunes on your PC about your device being in recovery mode.

How to Repair iPhone Wi-Fi Problems

If you notice slow *Wi-Fi* speed or a rise in dropped contacts, below are a few things you can test before contacting customer service.

Before you begin fiddling with your iPhone 14 settings, you'll desire to investigate if the *Wi-Fi* connection is giving you problems. If you're on your home Wi-Fi system, try unplugging the router for a moment before plugging it back in.

If you're sure it's not the router, you might like to check and find out if other people with the same ISP are experiencing similar issues locally.

If you can't access the router your cell phone is linked to, or if you're sure the problem has nothing to do with the connection with your ISP/router, go to your iPhone 14 Settings *app*.

Once you're here, you'll need to check the Wi-Fi system if you're having problems. Here's how exactly to do this:

1. In Settings, tap *Wi-Fi*.

2. Choose your connection by tapping the "*i*" in the circle.

3. Tap *Forget this Network* near the top of the display. (**Note:** This can trigger the request for your Wi-Fi password in your iPhone.)

If this doesn't function, try resetting your iPhone's system settings:

1. Head to your *Settings app*.

2. Tap *General*.

3. Tap *Reset Tap on* Reset Network Settings.

How to Repair iPhone Network Problems

If your iPhone suddenly displays a *"No Service"* symbol, and you also can't hook up to your cellular network, here are some steps to take.

1. First, ensure that there is no current outage in the area. Check social media for reviews and/or create a social media connection with your company. You can even test the network signal to see if others in your area are experiencing similar problems.

2. If you notice that the problem is unrelated to a system outage, you'll need to restart your iPhone to see if it resolves the issue.

3. If that doesn't work, try turning on Airplane Mode for 30 seconds before turning it off.

If you still can't get it to work normally, you should try turning off Cellular Data completely. Here's what you should do to get there:

1. Navigate to Settings.

2. Select Cellular.

3. Turn off Cellular Information.

4. Toggle it off for one minute, then back on.

How to Fix iPhone Sound Issues

Your iPhone speakers should produce clear, loud audio. However, if your audio starts to crackle or muffle, here are some things you can try before contacting Apple customer service again.

1. To begin, restart your iPhone. Additionally, ensure that

your SIM card is properly positioned in the holder. The new iPhone's SIM card slot is located on the left side of the device.

2. You can also experiment with turning Bluetooth connectivity on and off.

3. If the sound from the phone is still missing or distorted, make sure no particles are blocking the loudspeaker grille or the Lightning slot.

4. Restart your phone if you notice an abrupt drop in contact high quality. You should also inspect the device's recipient to ensure it is not obstructed by particles or your display screen protector if you have one. You can even try removing your situation if you're using one to see if that helps.

5. If your phone's microphone suddenly stops working or begins arbitrarily eliminating, try restarting it.

6. If the mic continues to be busted, you can test restoring your phone from the backup. If repairing doesn't function, you'll need to get in contact with Apple as you may have a hardware problem.

How to Repair iPhone Battery Life

Many iPhone users are usually enjoying excellent battery life. Nevertheless, some are beginning to notice the battery drains faster than its expected rate.

In case your *iPhone* battery life starts draining faster than it should, there are a few steps you need to take before contacting *Apple* support.

Using the *iPhone* several users worldwide, we would need to get feedback about their performance.

Most of the suggestions continue to be great.

We haven't seen widespread issues about battery existence (*not yet, at the very least*). However, many users say their battery is draining faster than it should.

Battery life problems are normal (particularly after Apple releases a brand-new *iOS* software program), and we realize that 5G drains batteries faster than *LTE,* so these complaints aren't anything serious to worry about.

If you begin noticing severe battery drain, you can take a few actions to resolve the problem. In this book section, we'll get you through some fixes that may help you repair poor iPhone battery life.

They are fixes that have worked for all of us over time, and they will help you solve your battery issues in moments and assist you in avoiding a talk session with *Apple customer support.*

Restart Your Phone. **If your battery starts draining faster than you imagine it should, we always recommend restarting your cell phone before doing other things.**

Power off your *iPhone*, wait one minute and power it ON again. If it's draining quickly, move ahead to the other steps below.

Update Your iPhone. Apple periodically releases software updates for the iPhone. Point updates (x.x.x) are usually focused on mending bugs, whilst milestone improvements (x.x) usually deliver a variety of functions and fixes.

The company may not call out battery fixes within an iOS update's change log, but new *firmware* always gets the potential to help alleviate battery issues greatly.

What to Do When Your iPhone Screen is Frozen

Several factors can freeze the screen of your device. The frozen screen can easily be solved by carrying out a hard reset. This can be achieved by holding the Power and Home buttons together until the Apple logo appears and disappears or until the screen turns black.

How to Repair iPhone Overheating Problems

We've seen the reviews about *iPhone* models getting hot through the setup, even operating apps, and providers like *GPS*. If you don't need to get your phone right into a store, here are some things to try out.

First, try removing the affected app (if you're using one) and find out if that helps. You'll also need to try turning the mobile phone Off and On. You can even try putting the mobile phone into *Airplane Setting*.

To Troubleshoot the Software, Hard Reset your iPhone by holding the Power and Home buttons together for 10 seconds. You will notice the Apple logo disappears. A software crash is the most common cause of your battery's failure to charge. If you still keep experiencing the same problem, check the cable frames for discoloration. Use another charging cable to charge it and check for any differences.

If it still doesn't work, clean the charging port with a clean toothbrush dipped in methylated spirit.

Tips and Tricks

Taking Screenshots

Screenshots are one way to make a copy of your screen for later use or to share with others.

Take a Screenshot Here is how to take a screenshot on your iPhone.

1. Open the content you want to screenshot.

2. At the same time, press the volume up button and the side button.

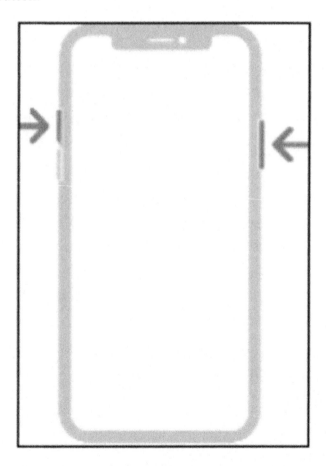

3. Your screen will flash immediately, and your screenshot will be ready.

Screenshots can be edited and viewed. Your screenshots are saved automatically in the Photos app. To edit or view your screenshots, follow the steps below:

1. In the Photos app, select Albums.

2. Tap Screenshots to see all the screenshots you've taken on your phone.

3. View, favorite, share or edit a screenshot by clicking on it.

4. Tap the camera icon or the Edit menu to add screenshots to apps like Messages or Mail.

Animoji and Memoji

Memoji and Animoji are innovative ways to convey messages. You can create a video message (maximum of 30 seconds)/ animated emoji characters by using the front-facing TrueDepth camera. These stickers are also applicable to Animojis. Although the Memojis are fixed, approximately 24 varieties in the settings allow you to select the specific emotion you want to display and a plethora of customization options.

Make a Memoji

1. Open the Messages app, join an existing conversation, or compose a new message.

2. Tap the Memoji button on the Message app drawer. If it's not visible, tap the App store icon to display it.

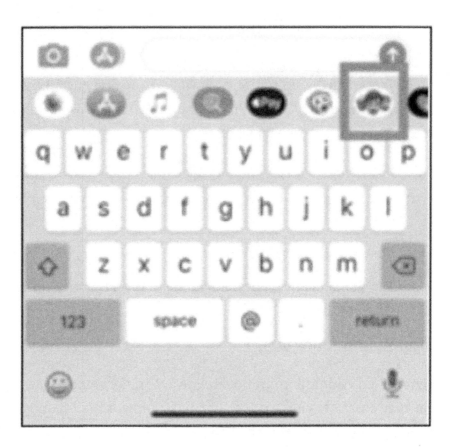

3. You will find several Animoji options to choose from.

4. Swipe right on the app drawer until you get to the end. Tap the Plus icon to view a blank Memoji canvas.

5. Tap each category, like color, skin, hairstyle, etc., and customize the Memoji as you wish.

6. Tap *Done* to save your settings.

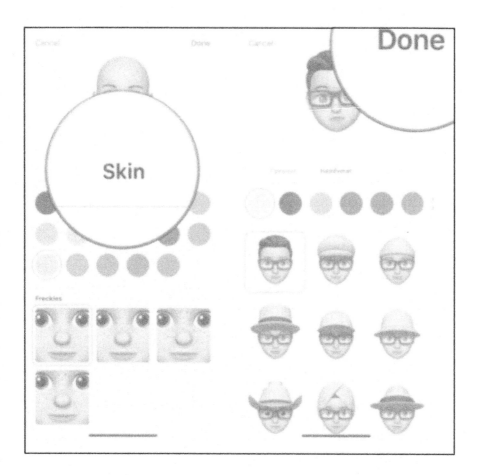

Edit a Memoji

1. Open a new message in the *Messages* app.

2. Tap the Memoji button ⊙ on the Message app drawer. If it's not visible, tap the App store icon to display it.

3. Scroll through all the available Memoji until you find the one you like, then click on it.

4. Tap the 3-dot icon at the top of your screen.

5. Tap *Edit*.

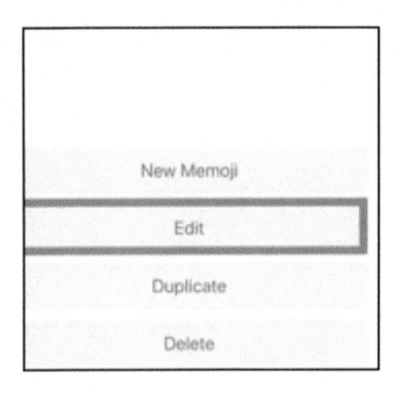

New Memoji

Edit

Duplicate

Delete

6. Scroll through the options on the next screen and customize the Memoji as it suits you.

Record and Send Animoji

1. Launch the *Messages* app, open an existing conversation or start a new message.

2. Tap the Animoji button 🐶 on the Message app drawer. If it's not visible, tap the App store icon to display it.

3. Swipe left to select your preferred Animoji character.

4. Select the record button ●. To stop recording, tap ■ .

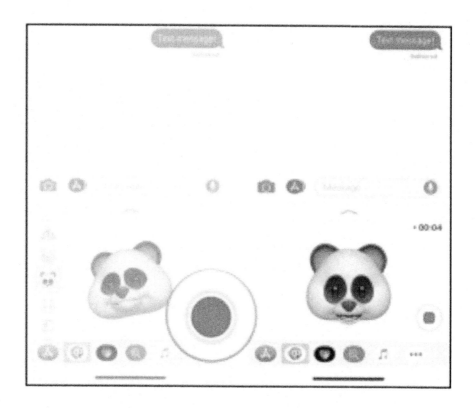

5. To delete this recording, select 🗑 .

6. Once done recording, tap send ⬆ .

Using Memoji Stickers

1. Launch the messaging app of your choice.

2. Tap 🐵 on your keyboard.

3. Scroll through the displayed list and click on any sticker pack you like.

4. Select the desired sticker.

5. Tap  to send.

Share Animoji to Social Networks

1. Launch the *Messages* app.

2. Open the conversation that has the Animoji or Memoji you wish to share.

3. Tap the Animoji.

4. Tap

5. Click on the social network or app that you want to share the Animoji.

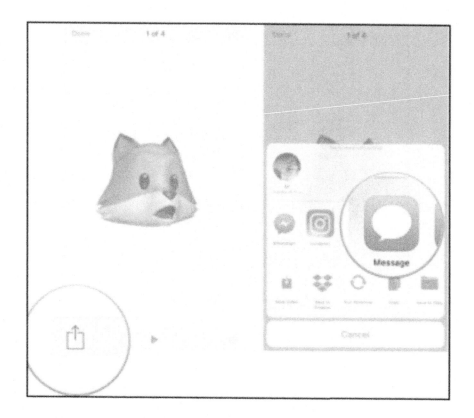

6. Then tap ⬆ to send.

Save an Animoji to Your Camera Roll

Follow the steps below to save an Animoji in the same way you save videos:

1. Launch the *Messages* app.

2. Open the conversation that has the Animoji or Memoji you wish to save.

3. Tap the Animoji.

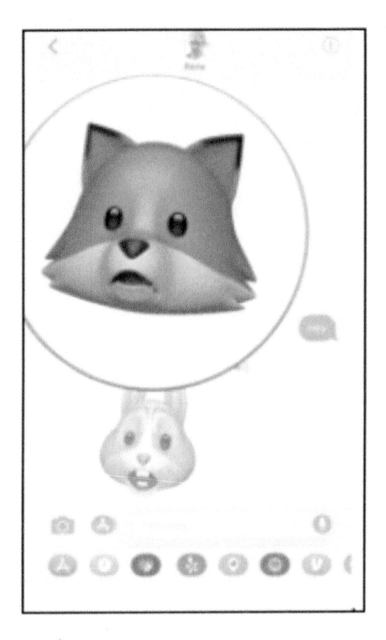

4. Tap 📤

5. *Then tap* Save Video.

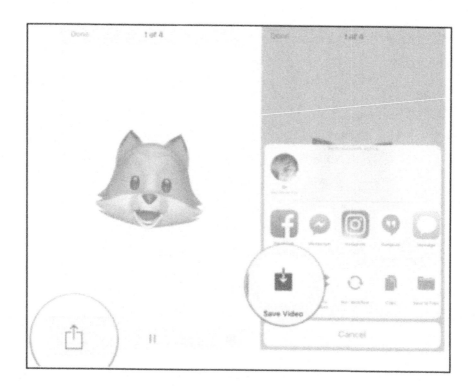

Share Saved Animoji from Camera Roll

Follow the steps above to save an Animoji as a video, then follow the steps below to share the Animoji from your camera roll.

1. Click on the *Videos* album in the *Photos* app.

2. Tap the saved Animoji video.

3. Tap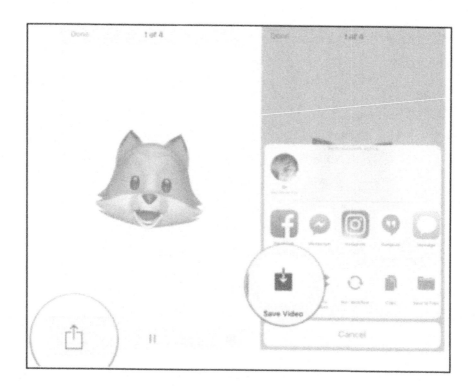

4. Click on the social network or app that you want to share the Animoji.

5. Tap *Post* to share the video.

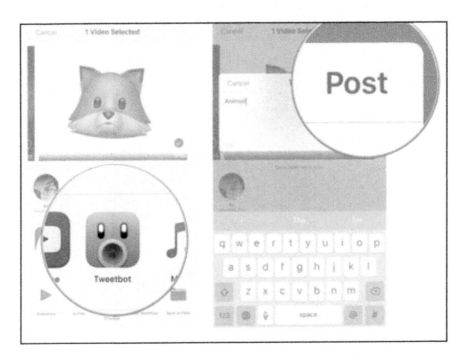

6. Turn a live picture into Bounce, Loop, and Long Exposure

7. Another iOS 15 feature allows you to convert live pictures into Bounce, Loop, & Long Exposure in the Photos application. After taking a live photo, touch the little downward arrow beside it to change it to Bounce, Loop, or Long Exposure.

Moving through Pages

Another great new feature that has been added to iOS 15, which was removed on iOS 14, is the ability to move through the pages simply by tapping your device's dock. Tap left or right to move between the pages on the home screen.

Add Multiple Faces to Face ID

If you want to register multiple faces to unlock your phone, follow these steps.

1. Select the Settings app.

2. As you scroll down, click Face ID & Passcode.

3. Please enter your password.

4. Touch Make another appearance.

5. Scan your face and follow the on-screen instructions.

Measure Objects With Your iPhone

You can never find the right meter whenever you need to measure something. Fortunately, you can measure parts and objects with your iPhone's built-in measurement tool. It's not perfect, but it's a useful tool for simultaneously measuring an object or the distance between two things. Take the following steps:

1. Start the measurement app.

2. Move your iPhone around so that the device can scan the surroundings.

3. Position your iPhone so the camera can point at the object you want to measure.

4. Move your iPhone until a white circle with a dot appears in the center.

5. Align the white point with the edge of the object to be measured.

6. Hold down the white button with the + sign.

7. Scroll to the item's opposite edge.

8. Hold the white button with the + sign down.

9. The application will display the approximate measurement.

Limit iPhone Use to Screen Duration

Are you guilty of using your iPhone excessively? Screen Time is a simple way to reduce time spent on social media, online shopping, and title scanning. The following are the steps to enable the clock on the screen:

1. Select the Settings app.

2. Now select Screen Time.

3. Then, select Application Limits.

4. Then select Add limit.

5. Select a category.

6. Select Add.

7. Select a time.

8. To save, hold down the top left arrow.

Configure Your Email Or Web Browser

Yes, Apple is finally relinquishing some control over its default apps. Currently, the feature is only available in email clients and web browsers. So, for example, you can map your browser or Outlook, where you will use Chrome as your preferred email app.

CONCLUSION

Thank you for reading this book. Apple's high-end iPhone 14 models live up to their moniker.

The iPhone 14 handbook can be extremely beneficial to owners. The handbook may contain the bare minimum of instructions for configuring applications and using the phone.

It was a pleasure to write this guide for you. I hope you found it useful and insightful.

Understanding the iPhone 14 user manual in its entirety is critical. The instructions will teach you how to use your new phone. It will also give you the instructions you need to use your iPhone. Knowing how to get the most out of your new phone is extremely beneficial. You shouldn't have to spend a lot of money. This handbook can also be used to figure out how to unlock it. Its features will astound you.

This comprehensive manual contains tips and tricks for both beginners and seniors to learn how to use their iPhone 14 like a pro.

The manual is intended for beginners, experts, and users transitioning from Android and Windows phones to Apple iPhones for the first time.

To improve the user's experience and skills, the manual has been organized with pictures and step-by-step instructions.

This iPhone 14 manual is a fantastic resource for the owner. The manual can provide basic information on using your phone and setting up applications.

A legitimate PDF for the device can also be found. A legal PDF ensures that it does not violate laws and will work with your phone. You can also keep track of authorized iPhone files. That way, you'll be reading them legally, which will benefit your trading practices. It is critical to have a thorough understanding of the iPhone 14 manual.

The manual will help you use your new phone. You'll also get basic tips on how to get the most out of your iPhone. Understanding how to get the most out of your new phone is extremely valuable. Good luck!

BONUS

**SCAN THE QR CODE BELOW TO GET
YOUR FULL COLOR VERSION PDF
OF THIS BOOK!**

SCAN THE QR CODE BELOW TO GET YOUR BONUS BOOK "MACBOOK SENIORS GUIDE" FULL COLOR VERSION PDF!

Printed in Great Britain
by Amazon

18114745R00119